Even a Man Can Have a Broken Heart

Mary E. Gilder

Published by
MEG's Publishing

Copyright © 2014 by Mary E. Gilder

This is a work of non-fiction.

Book Cover Designed by Brion Sausser, brion@bookcreatives.com
Interior Designed by Jessica Tilles, jessica@twasolutions.com

ISBN: 978-0-9823844-1-1

Library of Congress Control Number: 2013913097

Books are available at quatity discounts. For information, please contact: MEG's Publishing, P.O Box 1555, Newark, California 94560.

My Literary Warriors

A tribute to the amazing team that unselfishly extended to me their time, insight, wisdom, and honesty as they sifted through the pages. I extend to you endless gratitude.

Airiel Quintana, Arthur Cossey, Chandra Brooks, CheyNaRey, Cheryl Curry, Christy Hollis, Donna Alexander, Demetrice Owens, Gladys Castillo-Feely, Jane Sweet, Juanita Venegas, Lady Gilder, Dr. Ronald Griffin, Russell Nelson, Renay Jackson, Rhonda Bland, Richard Russell, Ruby Quintana, Rushell Brown, Sandra Buchanan-Atwaters, Sherlon Hazley, Simone Utsey, Tara Hollis, Tiera Gilder, Thomas Johnson, Yvonne Hollis, Yvonne Lange, Zenaida Roy-Almario

ACKNOWLEDGMENTS

𝒥'm amazed at how time flies when you are walking in your destiny. It has been 3 ½ years since I published my first novel and I'm more grateful today than ever. I'm grateful to GOD for allowing me to connect with my assignment because so many depart without having made that vital connection. And as you instructed, my assignment is being utilized to empower, enlighten and bring about positive change. With that said:

To the Gilder Family Ray, Torry, Tiera and Marshana, thank you for not allowing me to veer away from what GOD has ordered me to achieve. My heart is consumed with appreciation, admiration and endless joy.

To my God Children, you make my heart smile: Cherina Booker, Isabella Betts, Zahava Hydel, Airiel Quintana, Jackson Radonski and Taylor Radonski.

To my mother Yvonne Hollis you continue to be my biggest cheer leader. Having your support means the world to me.

To my loving family and friends, you know who you are. The love and support you have extended is beyond what my soul can contain. Never underestimate the gratitude I hold in my heart for you. Never forget that it takes a village and you have been that and so much more within my life.

To my God Mother Mrs. Bettye Wright, your courage amazes me. Thank you for pushing me as a teen to grow and connect with my inner strength.

To my Aunts the "Queens"…you had me at hello!!! Rushelle Brown, Debra Norris, Diane Conley, Margaret Lewis, Carol Staton, Gussie Williams, Thelma Calloway, Nell Simpson, Cathy Callahan, Lois Williams, Paulette Jackson

My lovely Editors Joan Burke and Jessica Tilles, thank you for taking good care of me.

My cover designer Brion Sausser, "A Misrepresentation of Myself," currently sits in a Museum. Need I say more…You ROCK!!!

My assistant Airiel Quintana, we have accomplished so much in a short period of time and we've only just begun. You are simply brilliant.

Cyrus A. Webb, thank you for believing in my potential in various arenas. I'm forever grateful.

Thank you to my Literary Partner in Crime, author Sheryl Mallory Johnson. Yes, we are on this beautiful Literary Journey together and that is a blessing. Continue creating Literary Magic.

My Literary Mentor author-Renay Jackson, thank you for extending to me endless hours of wisdom. I have listened and digested each and every word.

My lifetime Mentor Dr. Patricia Worthy-Oyeshiku, it is because of you that I was moved to evolve into a better version of myself. I have said it once and I will repeat these words until the day I depart from this earth, "you are something very special."

Lifetime Mentor Dr. Ronald Griffin, thanks for standing on the frontline with me during my Graduate studies and beyond. Continuously, reminding me that I'm deserving of all GOD has willed to be.

TO THE WOMEN WHO KEEP ME GROUNDED: Thank you for ensuring that I stay focused on my assignment. Many of you have stood on the frontline with me for what feels like a lifetime. Your love and support comes with no condition and that is a beautiful blessing. My heart is filled with endless gratitude

Cynthia Betts, Tasha Biship, Cheryl Curry, Dr. Gloria Carreon, Gladys Castillo-Feely, Tiera Gilder, Marshana Gilder, Terri Glave, Gloria Ifil, Thelmon Jackson, Lora Kent, Zela Ocon, Adrienne Sierra, Jane Sweet, Donielle Turner, Simone Utsey and Juanita Venegas, Tracy Harbin, Yvonne Hollis

My Heros

$\mathcal{V}$ernessa Baker, Michael Green, Maria Rolon, Vonda Stanford and all of the patients receiving treatment at MD Anderson Cancer Research Hospital.

DEDICATED TO MY REMARKABLE NEPHEWS

You are Brilliant, Courageous, Resilient, Compassionate and Loving. And as you continue your journey, be mindful that you are here for a moment. Your stay may feel like an eternity, but it's only a moment. And being knowledgeable of that truth…keep GOD first. In addition, love deeply and passionately; be unafraid in asking for what it is you desire and treasure every moment of your life:

Jace Brown, La Mar Chapman, Jamond Curry, Eddie Fobbs Jr., Eric Fobbs, Eric Fobbs Jr., Spencer Foreman, Jasmone Halbert, Julian Hobdy, Jonathan Holden, Robert Holden, Theaudeus Holden, Brandon Ifil, Devon Ifil, Denarian McCants, Gabriel McCants, Zar Norris, Kerwin Owens, Devin Owens, Richard Russell Jr., David Russell, Fransua Senegal, Fransua Senegal Jr., Danny Smith, Ronald Smith, Morris Brown, Danny MacKenetti, J'Moryn Freeman, and De Anthony Burgess

"When you look in life's mirror ask yourself, am I who I proclaim to be. When you look in life's mirror, do you recognize the image staring back at you or are you simply wearing a well designed mask? Honesty with others is important, however honesty with self vital."

— Mary E. Gilder

PROLOGUE

As a small child I can remember a grand event taking place for what appeared to occur one Friday per month when mother's friends would come to our home around 10:00 pm for Girl Friend Social Time. I can recall the big hair, beautiful figures, glossy lips, sexy clothes, warm smiles and lots of laughter. My curiosity heightened from what took place in the family kitchen around 12:00 am. My mother would fry fish, chicken or make tacos. And while sipping on wine, they would listen to Marvin Gaye, Teddy or some other sex symbol as they engaged in deep discussion about life, love, heartbreak, regrets, etc. Most importantly, they talked about their individual journey as it pertained to men and the numerous life lessons learned. Even though I was ordered to bed, I would sit as quiet as a mouse with my bedroom door slightly open as I tuned in to every word exchanged. Lessons and life instructions unbeknownst to them, a powerful gift bestowed unto me.

Many years later, this same ritual would play out within my home. Several times per year the women within my life would gather at my home for what we viewed as Girl Friend Therapy. I would prepare a small feast consisting of gumbo, potato salad, collard greens, cornbread, peach cobbler, vanilla ice cream and pound cake. And while indulging on delicious cuisine, all in attendance would sit around the dining room table and talk about life. Within this group a high level of trust and respect existed and like a game of craps, issues were tossed on the table; issues pertaining to love, passion, marriage, divorce, new relationships, regrets, our hopes and successes. In addition, some sought advice, direction, wisdom and support. Even though the stories varied, one commonality prevailed—our inability as women to understand loves manifestation in the soul of a man. How did love look and feel to the men in our lives, at the profoundest level?

INTRODUCTION

For numerous years, I have shared conversations with countless women representing various ethnicities, cultures and social economic levels. And an overwhelmingly commonality shared is a belief that some men lack the capacity to love deeply.

Even a Man Can Have a Broken Heart was written as a tool to help increase women's understanding as it pertains to love's many complexities from a male's perspective. Also, the goal of this book is to help men gain insight into how their experiences, past and present, may have a direct impact on decisions made each and every day. I interviewed five amazing men and each made an attempt to identify and disclose the various factors, both positive and negative, that have made an impact on their ability to commit, trust, and love profoundly.

For the purpose of this work, it is not my goal to spend in-depth time assessing my theories that support a particular stance or belief system. However, I will reveal my stance, which supports the belief that men indeed have the capacity to love just as profoundly as women and do. The way in which their love may manifest and present itself may differ and vary from culture to culture.

My take is that we were all sent here to learn many life lessons and that our greatest challenge is to tap into what it is our soul desires and to learn how to open our hearts to love. This is the challenge.

I could go on and on, but the sole purpose of this book is to explore the thoughts of my readers and in doing so, I presented a thought-provoking question to a random group of women—women representing various cultures, ethnicities and social economic levels.

The question was presented and the responses poured in. I present to you the question: *Do you feel that men have the capacity to love profoundly?*

CHAPTER ONE
The Letters

The following letters represent a canvas displaying the responses to the question. The responses are directed not only at the question's presenter, but also at America's men.

Mary,

My experience has been that when you let loose with those three little words, "I love you," he can't wait to run and will give a list as to why you aren't right for him.

The first love of my life, a beautiful free spirit, left me in a heap of tears at college. I had just lost my virginity to a total jerk and met this man who treated me so well. He touched my soul. He was a virgin and I became his teacher. I, the recent former virgin, was teaching him the ways of love. We talked about living together when we went to graduate school in a year. He went home for a summer, leaving me with the visions of our future together.

When he returned, there was no call to me. I see him on campus, he wants to talk and I think that he is going to want to live together now. No. I get this "list." He doesn't want to be with me because I am not "politically aware enough, not independent enough, etc..." I found out from a girlfriend that during the summer, he went back to his old girlfriend, now that he was an experienced lover.

The second love of my life also had his list. We worked together and developed a loving relationship. He would feed me strawberries that he picked off the bush for me. We spent nearly every waking and sleeping moment together. I would cheer for him at our office softball games. We spent so much time together that we were practically living together. I told him that I loved him and he told me that he could see us married in five years. My heart and mind were flying. Then later he told me that I wasn't athletic enough for him, etc. and he didn't want to be with me anymore.

So, you tell me how a man can love profoundly when he treats the woman who he appears to love this way. I think that it's crazy to think that a man can love as deeply when he can so easily toss aside women that he loves because he is too afraid to commit. Mary, are you out of your ever-lovin' mind?

Still waiting,

Janice

No Mary,

Most men don't have the capacity to love profoundly because many lack the capacity to trust—trust at a level that allows one to express what's truly in their hearts. Many would rather silence their words and allow their actions to speak for what's in their heart. As a result, an environment of utter confusion is manifested as women are forced to rely on their own understanding in an attempt to figure the shit out. And probably 80% of the time, our conclusions are wrong. However, this is the insanity placed upon us.

Recently, a male relative shared with me his regrets. For the sake of confidentiality in this letter, I will refer to him as "Jake" and her as "Kim." He met this young lady at an art exhibit and described her simply as remarkable. They had been dating for several months when he decided that a weekend alone at a beachfront resort would be nice.

Kim arrived a day in advance to relax and prepare for him. Jake stated that on the morning of his flight he woke with a tremendous amount of guilt because he was still living with his wife. Jake and his wife had filed for divorce and slept in separate rooms. However, he failed to share that information with Kim because he knew she would have never explored a relationship with a married man. Jake stated that shame and guilt did not permit him to join her or call to explain his absence. He said as minutes turned to hours and hours into days, he became too scared to answer his cell. His solution was to turn it off. Weeks passed before he responded to her numerous messages. He shared how he allowed his actions to represent his words, which forced her to rely upon her own understanding.

When they finally spoke months later, Kim revealed to him that she had cried off and on for weeks, never understanding why Jake didn't show or call to simply explain. Instead, he allowed her to suffer unnecessarily. Jake said he was surprised to hear her say that she felt that this did not reflect his character and assumed something pretty dreadful must have happened. She said that all he had to do was simply provide an explanation. Yes, disappointment would have followed, but the clarity would have eased her pain.

Mary, I believe that many times the best of men are viewed as jerks because they lack the courage to speak from their hearts. Most appear to have no problem with communicating on a superficial level. However, until men learn to peel away the various layers and speak from their souls, they will be unable to offer a well-deserving woman the very best within them.

Jake stated that his cowardliness caused him to lose Kim, a woman he had fallen in love with.

Mary, the complexities of the male species appear to be far beyond the intellectual scope of most women. Most of us are on Prozac just trying to deal with their baggage.

— Anne Marie

Mary,

Yes, Mary, men do have the capacity to love on a profound level but only with their dicks. When they see a beautiful woman, their dicks start to inflate like inner tubes in their pants and their minds start to figure out how they are going to catch that fine piece of specimen.

It's very rare that you find a man who can love unselfishly, unconditionally and profoundly. Well, just maybe, if he's old, bored, broke down and ain't-nothing-working-no-more, then he'll give unselfishly and unconditionally for some companionship

Finally, are men emotionally numb to love? Well, not if they first learn to love themselves. I believe the problem is most [men] don't apply the needed energy required to gain a positive relationship with their soul. Before, I would always hear people say, "Learn to love yourself." I never gave it much thought, but when I actually applied it to myself, I became fulfilled. I realize that everyone needs love, but I also believe that if men stop being controlled by what's between their legs, everything would fall into place. There's always love out there. Men need to be emotionally strong, trust in themselves, be genuine, and let Mother Nature take her place.

Much love,
Vanessa

Dear Mary,

First, I must apologize for the late response. I have pondered over these questions for weeks. Let me first begin by explaining where I am spiritually, emotionally and physically. I ended a relationship with a man who I thought *was my soul mate, a man that God had sent into my life. I never thought that he would cheat on me, but he did... repeatedly. I thought that he loved me with all his mind, body and soul, as I did him. I was devastated that he could step out on our relationship, and even more devastated that he lied about it.*

Do men have the capacity to love profoundly? I want to believe in the depths of my soul that men can love profoundly, but can they really? But then I ask myself, do women have the capacity to love on that level? I think that in order to love profoundly, one has to first love God. God is the best example of love. He laid down his life so that we may have life everlasting. How many people could say that they would lay down their lives for the ones they love and actually commit the act? How does one love unselfishly when we live in a society where we worship envy and competition; competing for riches, fame, the biggest home on the block, the trophy wife/husband, etc.?

I am a young woman and now it appears that I don't know much when it comes to life and love. I thought I knew it all. I sometimes ask myself, "Is it supposed to be this hard? Is it supposed to be this difficult?" My thought is that love is an unconditional state, but what is one to do when it comes with a condition?

Can a man love unselfishly? That is a hard question as well. Hmm, what does it mean to love unselfishly? Is it not wanting to change something about your significant other? Is it learning to love him or her as they are? In order to answer this question, I wanted to be sure that I had a real understanding of the word unselfishly. I understand it to mean love generously, to love forsaking oneself and giving to another. Wow. I am not even sure if I have the capacity to do that because I walk around guarded. My current life mission is to guard my heart. How do you live like you've never been hurt? How can one truly forsake oneself when, as I said previously, we live in a materialistic society?

I say yes, men can love unselfishly and do have the capacity to love profoundly. This is my hope, my desire and my blessing—to find a man who is able to love profoundly and unselfishly. In the same breath, I desire to give of myself as this man will of himself, as we come together in union. Is this a fairytale or a pipe dream? I certainly hope not. So when I get the chance to sit it out or dance, I hope I dance. (Dance by Lee Ann Womack).

Mary, I do believe that men have the capacity to love profoundly. Have I ever been a recipient of such profoundness? Hmm, not as of yet.

— Karla

❧

Dear Mary,

Last week I was at my sister's wedding and while at the reception this guy came up to me and started a conversation. He was extremely attractive and appeared to be highly intelligent. I was pleased with our conversation. That was until he threw me for a loop by asking me if I was married. His question shocked me because he was the one wearing a wedding band. I thought that I would put him on the hot seat by turning the question on him.

He refused to give me a response and I asked him repeatedly. Finally, he defended himself by stating that he was asking me if I were married out of respect for my husband. Well, I explained that my request of him was out of respect for his wife. I needed him to respond to my question and he refused. His behavior represents that of so many men, regardless of ethnicity or culture. Yes, we women share our various stories. I believe that most men expect to be shared by many, but they refuse to share with another man. It's perfectly okay for women to betray their values, but the thought of men compromising theirs is not an option, a subject not open for discussion.

In my honest opinion, most men are selfish and don't possess the capacity to love profoundly because they refuse to address the many issues crippling their hearts.

Mary, you know that I have nothing but love for you, but when it comes to this topic, keep dreaming.

Sincerely,

Victoria

Mary,

Of course men can love as profoundly, if not more [than women]. Men are also emotional creatures. It's just that our society has made it difficult for men to express their emotions, much less their inner and soul-gripping feelings. "It's not manly," or "Men need to be the tough ones," our society demands.

Before a woman came into this world, wasn't it Adam who first sought out love, he who was extremely lonely? He knew something was missing in his life. He yearned for another being to share all the beauty and goodness that surrounded him, someone to communicate with, to hold, to touch...to complete him.

There are many forms of love. It began with the greatest love that God has for us, his children, the Agape, unconditional love. We adopted this love and extended it to our own offspring, our precious children. There is also the love and respect for our parents, our brothers and sisters, our neighbors and our loyalty to our country. Then there is the love that our loving God has designed only to be experienced between a man and a woman. I feel that this is the deepest kind of love. It is where we can express our love using all five of our senses. When we love, we experience a natural high and never want to come down, but we eventually do.

And yet there's even a greater love much deeper and incomprehensible, the kind where both people seek each other's true makeup—what's in their hearts and their souls— and then accepts everything, the good and the bad about each other. When two people experience this euphoric love, problems seem smaller, energy levels are higher, smiles and laughter come easier and food tastes better. This is the kind of love that makes the world round.

I personally have been fortunate to experience this kind of deep love from a very special man. This kind of love is rare and is as valuable as life itself. He sees my flaws and inadequacies, including my imperfect past and imperfect family. He adores me from head to toe and makes me feel like I am the most beautiful creature that walked this earth. He has displayed sincere kindness, infinite patience and an outpouring love that cannot be contained. He is my best friend, my rock, my hero, my inspiration. We share our dreams and passions as well as our failures. We have stimulating and lengthy conversations. We cherish every moment together. We laugh, we cry, and we bring out the best in each other. I totally trust him and I have no doubts of his love for me. He always reminds me that I am his gift from heaven. I can honestly say that we "both" love each other deeply, completely and unconditionally.

Yes, Mary, men possess the capacity to love profoundly and deeply.

Sincerely,

Guinevere

My Sister Mary,

Who are these men that you are talking about? Let me tell you, sista, they always talking that shit about, "I want a good woman," when for real, if one walked up and slapped his face, his ass wouldn't even know what slapped his dumb ass. Love? No, they want SEX.

LOVE and PASSION for men = SEX, plain and simple. I am convinced that love and passion to a man are defined as sex and that is about as deep as it gets. They are not looking for LOVE; they want sex without commitment and they want it with the masses. And for real, most of the time it isn't all that good. In order to love profoundly, you must be willing to become vulnerable and also be just as willing to make a commitment.

Dudes just do not seem to be interested in the "C" word much. They just seem to think that quantity is what makes a man. They totally forget that one day them little ding-a-lings of theirs are gonna wear out and stop working and then what are they going to have? They totally forget about the "Q" word— quality.

LOVE until it hurts? No, they want SEX until it hurts.

So Mary, I think that you are wrong and the answer to your question, in my opinion, is absolutely no, no, no and no.

— Tashara

Dear Mary,

The answer to your question is yes, most definitely yes! Men do have the capacity to love just as profoundly as women do but in their own way and on their own time. The men who I have encountered or even questioned about their ability to allow themselves to fall in love, or even just simply love, all answered in a similar way: "Yes, I know how to love, but have I found the right one is the question that remains unanswered."

I believe that there are many men who have indeed been in love, but their timing wasn't right. By timing, I mean they were not ready to settle down or wanted to see what else was out there or...that list can certainly go on.

I once heard that a woman meets a man and then falls in love. Men, on the other hand, say I am ready to fall in love and then go searching for that someone, special or not. Some men's ability to grab hold of a good thing when it is in hand's reach can be non-existent. It is not until that special someone has walked out of that man's life does he realize that maybe that one was indeed the one. The unfortunate thing is, by the time the man realizes that they were in love, one of two things usually occurs. One, it is too late because their significant other has moved on or is fed up with waiting for them. The other is that their ego or pride gets in the way, telling them that this wasn't the one anyway and that someone else is soon to follow.

So Mary, you ask if men have the capacity to love as deeply as women do and the answer is yes, but in their own way and on their own time. Just keep in mind their time and way may not be in line with the significant other that is currently in their life.

— Ashlie

CHAPTER TWO
The Men: An Overview and Profiles

The same question was posed to several men and a small sample agreed to share their words. They willfully shared their experiences with various aspects of love so that we could possibly attain a higher level of enlightenment. The information in the following chapters is presented in the form of intense interviews with five men: Zack, Brion, Ethan, Zayven and Drayke.

The best way to describe the interviews is to simply say powerful, powerful because of the level of profoundness. The interview process provided participants with a safe forum to remove their masks as they peeled away years of emotional, protective armor, allowing the interviewer to gain a glimpse into their souls as they recounted their various issues pertaining to how they love, their hopes, fears, pain, sorrows, regrets, passions and their dreams. Something women have been trying to decipher for centuries.

Each participant also shared the consequences stemming from the various choices they have made. During the very candid discussions, participants also revealed the role one's family of origin played in influencing how their love manifests.

All five men utilized the interviewer as a tool to aid them in opening their hearts to the world, so that readers will be inspired and challenged to reassess their own love language.

Ethan

CHAPTER THREE
Could Only Love on a Certain Level

Zodiac Sign: Cancer
Approximate Age: Forties
Occupation: Business Manager
Passion: Christ, studying the word and
interacting with people
Hobbies: Tinkering with cars, restoring old
vehicles, reading and basketball

"I think that in most of my relationships, the women put in way more effort than I did. When I say that, I'll say she put more effort emotionally, more feelings into it. I'll say all of the women that I've been with and been committed to in a relationship have loved me more than I loved them, with the exception of the first relationship [in which] I think we were equal. It's difficult for me to explain why. I think after

the first relationship it was just hard for me to put my all into a relationship.

I feel like they loved me more. I don't know why. It just became difficult for me to love. I could love on a certain level. I mean, when it came to giving an equal amount of love, that I could not do." — Ethan

"What were your thoughts about love before the age of twenty-one?"

What were my thoughts about love before the age of twenty-one? Well, I think what I thought it was, was riding a bus or riding my bike across town or walking across town to see my girlfriend, not realizing that it would take two to three hours to do so. Umm, and disobeying my parents to go see her. It's a difficult question because I wasn't taught what to do when I met a girl at that age. My dad didn't teach me. He didn't tell me what would happen or how I was going to feel.

Growing up with four sisters in the house, I saw their boyfriends and how they treated them. Me being the youngest, I learned a lot from everybody. But, I really didn't think much about love at that age. I didn't know what it was. All I knew was I liked this girl and I would do anything to go see her. I thought it was not worrying about whether somebody had a car; riding the bus with them was okay. I didn't worry about the clothes I wore at times. I just wanted to be accepted for who I was. But then there were times when I did want to be accepted because of what I had on, because everybody else was looking the part. I don't know. It's difficult to flash back because I wasn't in love at the time, although I had a girlfriend.

"Even though you had not connected with love at that point in time, those gushy feelings that you felt, what did that feel like? Did your heart flutter?"

I mean, emotionally I got butterflies around the person. I was nervous. I would spill drinks and trip over the carpet. I mean, I would do that stuff in hopes that I wouldn't do it. Trying so hard not to do it, I would still do something goofy, you know? I could also tell that she would be careful around me too. But at the same time, I've always been an… I can't say. I didn't take the lead at that time. I would wait for her to make the move. I got butterflies when I was on the phone. I didn't know what to say. I found myself being, you know, quiet during conversations on the phone because I was trying to be careful. I didn't want to say the wrong thing because I thought that she would be a keeper. But at the same time, other than the butterflies, I don't know.

"When a relationship didn't work, what did that feel like as a young man?"

When some didn't work out, my feelings would be hurt, especially if I liked the girl. I would be crushed. I thought I had to learn more. I thought I had to say more, do more, at least be better than the next guy. But I found myself not getting a girl, whereas my homeboy could. You know what I mean? As a matter of fact, I had a girlfriend in eighth grade that went with my best friend because she told everybody I didn't know how to kiss. At that age, [she was right] I didn't know how to kiss. She stuck her tongue in my mouth and I almost bit it off. I didn't know what was going on.

"How did that make you feel when you were just learning, at that age, society's expectations? Maybe it could have been your neighborhood's or family's expectations, but there was an expectation somewhere. How did you try to meet that expectation? Was there pressure?"

Yeah, I felt pressure. I mean, I even lied about having sex. I mean, because of my age, you know what I mean? I'm like I already done that, you know? Been there done that. I didn't want to say, "I'm seventeen, almost eighteen and I still haven't had sex, dude." I didn't want that embarrassment.

Umm, I don't know. It's just hard to say how I felt, because at that time it didn't matter to me whether I could get the girl or not. I just wasn't that interested in being in love at that time. It didn't bother me if my feelings got hurt. The next day I would shake it off. I'd be like, "Well, I guess I'll wait and see what happens with the next one that comes along." I mean, I guess at that age the attraction was different. The attraction at eighteen for me was, I hate to say this, but the attraction was to get a girl and to take her to bed. The attraction wasn't her mind; it was more or less her body and what she wanted to do sexually. So, it really wasn't love at all. It was more lust. I mean, even at that age, I'm thinking I'm in love, but it's really a lusting, because even after it happens, it's like, "Oh, it wasn't all that anyway," you know what I mean? But I don't know the feelings I got. I'd been rejected a couple of times at that age, and yeah it hurt. But like I said, it didn't hurt long.

"How were you raised to treat a woman?"

How I was raised to treat women? That's a tough question for me because how I was raised to treat them, what I was shown, and how I actually treated women was like night and day. Like I said, my dad was there but he wasn't. He treated my mother really bad, in a sense that he neglected her. So following my father's example of how to treat a woman would be totally the wrong way. I have four older sisters, and my mother, and she always says that I'm totally retro when it comes to treating a woman. I mean, I'm old-fashioned. I'll open the door. I'll make sure she gets into the house. I mean, I'll do all the things that a gentleman is supposed to do.

How I was raised to treat women was to respect them, not to call them names, not to talk about them. I've always known that women were self-conscious about appearance, about weight, and things like that. Like I said, watching, my mother and my sisters go through it, I've always known how sensitive a woman is, and I hated to see women cry. If there was one thing I never wanted to do is make a woman cry. I can't say I've been successful at that. But I was raised to respect women, to treat them like I wanted to be treated, just like I would treat anybody. I was definitely raised to treat women with respect, to treat all women like I wanted my mother to be treated. My mother was more or less my example. She was more or less the mother and father. My sisters, they more or less taught me how not to treat a woman by the guys they were with. I was more of an observer, but I was taught the basic things—not to hit them, not to talk about them, not to disrespect them or abuse them. That's more or less it.

"Can you recall when you first fell in love?"

When did I first fall in love? I have to say it had to be with my first girlfriend. I was eighteen or nineteen, even though I didn't know that's what it was. Later on I knew that's what it was because I wasn't interested in any other women at the time. I didn't feel like I had to cheat. I felt like I could get everything from her and focus my attention completely on her. She was more or less like the only woman in the room. So, I knew it was something other than just a feeling. I knew it was more than just me liking her because I would do anything to be with her. I would lie to be with her. She would lie to be with me. I knew I was in love with her. It's hard for me to say that because right now, looking back, it really didn't seem like I was in love. But at the time, I could say I was in love.

"Can you describe what love felt like?

It felt so good at times that I actually couldn't wait until the next day. I mean, I'd fall asleep on the phone, you know, things I wouldn't normally do. These were things I hadn't done with a woman before.

I ended up staying in that relationship for five years. And I also know that there is a thin line between that love and not being in love [because of] events that happened during that relationship. At the time, I unfortunately went to prison. I stayed about thirty to forty months, so about three and a half years. I was with this person up until I went, and when I got out it was totally different. I had to question myself about whether I was really in love with her or not. But I think I was. I think it was her willingness not to wait for me. When I saw her again, she had another child that I didn't know about. I'm saying these things because these are some of the things that prevented me from moving forward with other people.

"Did your prison time lessen the love in your heart for this woman?"

It subsided through tears. It subsided through her not responding the way I thought she should have. Not accepting the phone calls was the first sign. Also, not being at home for planned phone calls and not visiting. I mean, there was a lot of things that made my feelings subside. I talked to other guys who let me know, "Look, you may as well forget about that because she's already gone." Those were things I didn't want to hear, but I think it was easier for me to get away from it when I got out because I didn't have any feelings for her at all. I didn't. When I got out and I seen her, I think she tried to kiss me and I literally turned my head away because of a lot of things I heard that she did when I was in there. I mean, she was a drug addict when I got out, and to this day continues to be. That impacted our relationship. I think it may have been different if there hadn't have been another guy involved, another child involved, the drugs, but I think I was truly in love with her because it hurt so bad.

"Can you describe how your heart felt?"

The pain literally took my breath away. I literally felt like I didn't have my right hand anymore. I mean, she was like my right hand. It was like if you seen me, you seen her. If you seen her, you seen me. It's almost like it went from one extreme to the other, overnight. And I don't think I have ever felt pain like that before. That was like the worst. It made me cry. I mean, literally it made me boo-hoo. I tried to hold back the tears and I couldn't. I couldn't suppress them. So, it was real painful, knowing that I wouldn't have her anymore. It was like being powerless. I couldn't control the situation so that hurt too, and I had no control over it.

Having gone through the first relationship, it was a while before I got into another one because there was a kid involved. There was a kid without a mother or a father at the time, which is my son. He had his grandmother, who was the custodial parent. And at that time, I think he was three and his mama was gone. When I saw that child I said, "You know what? I can't leave this kid without a mother and a father." As much as I wanted to bounce, as much as I wanted to leave that situation for good and not even look back, I couldn't do it to the kid. Something moved me to say, "You know what? You're responsible for that child, so don't abandon him." *I* felt abandoned. I mean, I felt like his mom abandoned me and I wanted to abandon everything about her, including the kid.

"Tell me about your next relationship."

Now the next time I got into a relationship I was really careful. I was about 25. I moved to Oklahoma. I said, "Let me try a different scene. Let me try different people. Let me try to just start brand-new." In doing that, I ended up getting with the sister of my brother's girlfriend. Two brothers and two sisters; that's kind of common at times. She was younger than me, four or five years younger. So, I felt like I had to teach her and raise her and to more or less educate her on what I liked and how to treat a guy because she was, I felt, slow when it came to relationships. She was from a small country town and very inexperienced. She hadn't been to too many places, hadn't had but maybe one boyfriend. But my love for her came a little different.

It took a while. I think I hung out with her almost a year before I even decided I wanted to commit to any type of relationship. I think that in most of my relationships, the women put in way more effort than I have. When I say that, I'll say she put more effort emotionally, more feelings into it. I'll say all of the women that I've been with and been committed to in a relationship have loved me more than I loved them, with the exception of the first relationship [in which] I think we were equal. It's difficult for me to explain why. I think after the first relationship it was just hard for me to put my all into a relationship.

I feel like they loved me more. I don't know why. It just became difficult for me to love. I could love on a certain level. But when it came to giving an equal amount of love *that* I could not do.

It was more apparent back then in gift-giving and in visiting families on holidays. It was more apparent in her going out of her way to do things for me at times when I wouldn't go out of my way to do things. I was more or less unconcerned about her feelings, like if she was having a bad day or going through something outside of our relationship. I was more unconcerned than she was. I mean, when she was going through those "you know what, I'm not feeling good because me and my mom are not getting along" or "these people at my job are trippin'" moments, I was kind of unconcerned. I'd listen and then give maybe a one-word answer to a question or something.

"What would be her response to your lack of empathy?"

Well, I don't think she would get mad, but she would ask me things like, "Do you even care that I'm having a bad day?" And then unconsciously I would not respond. I mean, it would be like, "Oh yeah, I'm sorry. I didn't mean to ignore you." It may be that I was watching TV or mentally I was just somewhere else. You know what I mean? There was even times when I would respond with, "You know I got problems of my own." And at times, she didn't appear to care about what I was going through, so it was tit for tat at that point. It was like, "Well, when I talk to you about my issues, you don't seem to care." And I kind of followed the lead on that. But that's a pretty deep question because that's hard.

From the first relationship to the next, I guess I felt different because I didn't want this relationship to end up like the last one. I didn't want it to end up in heartbreak. I didn't want it to end in tears. I didn't want it to end on a bad note. Yeah, I think I was more protective of my feelings and of just letting my raw emotions go. I didn't want to be disappointed again. I think I more or less chose her, instead of her choosing me. I think I was more or less in control of that relationship. If it had been a stronger woman, she probably wouldn't have gone for some of those scenarios. I think my choice in women had kind of downgraded, to where if I did lose her, it wouldn't hurt that bad. It was a fun relationship. This is the first one I had experienced being cheated on. My first relationship, you know, there was no cheating at all. There was not even a thought of it. But this relationship, where my feelings had changed and there was a shift in emotions and stuff, other people got involved. I found myself losing control anyway. I think from there, all hell broke loose as far as me opening up to anyone.

She did cheat and I was angry but not angry enough to leave her. I was angry enough to ask questions. I wasn't angry enough to go after it, the dude, or to cause her any harm. I more or less said, "Well, this is my way out. I guess this one is over since we've gone there now. I guess this relationship is over and I'll just treat it how I want to now. I'll disrespect it if I want to and I'll get away with it because this is what she did." I more or less didn't look at the reasons why she did it. I just, more or less, looked at the fact that she did do it and I felt like I was disrespected. I didn't think that maybe it was something I did. I later on thought about it like, "Well, maybe I'm not giving her the love she deserves and maybe I underestimated this woman. And maybe she just said, "You know what, he thinks I'm going to sit here and wait on him to open up to me and treat me the way I want to be treated…" Even though I didn't treat her bad, I just wasn't attentive. I think I underestimated her.

I just want to back track a little bit about how I was taught to treat a woman. I did mention that I was taught to treat them with respect, but I was also taught visually and verbally how to disrespect a woman if I felt she was "out of line" or disrespecting me. This was taught by some of the older cats that I grew up with, like my cousins and brothers, who were more or less so-called pimps and players who ran the street. They treated a woman according to how they felt at any given moment. They followed the "gangsta manual." You know, a woman should stay in her place. She shouldn't speak unless spoken to. She shouldn't disrespect you in front of your boys and if so, you just, you know, smack her or check her. And that's more or less to back track on how I was raised to treat women. I was also taught how to disrespect them if needed.

Now, catching up to the second relationship, it's kind of important because it has a lot to do with my spirituality today. During this relationship, I was cheated on. In turn it made me look at it a lot differently in terms of my longevity in that relationship. It hurt a lot. I had mixed emotions about it. I think it hurt more than I said it did. I think I kind of suppressed some of the feelings I had because I was thinking, "You know what? Who is she? I can just get another woman." But at the same time, it hurt badly enough for me to wanna cry out and act out. I didn't want to do anything. I didn't want to physically harm her. I more or less wanted to hurt her feelings the way she hurt mine.

I ended up sleeping with one of her schoolmates, and she didn't take that well. I think she was hurt more than I was. That relationship wasn't really a relationship. I kind of slept with one of her friends, who in turn wanted to continue, and I didn't want to continue that. I ended up getting in a lot of trouble in that situation, as far as being hurt and then hurting other people's feelings. I mean, my feelings got hurt and I hurt someone's feelings, and then I hurt someone else's feelings. It kind of snowballed into a lot of people getting hurt. At the same time, I kind of wanted things to be back to normal and because they didn't, I ended up not wanting her to go anywhere by herself. I didn't trust her anymore. My level of trust in any woman had just gone away.

"Please expand on your perceptions as they pertain to your level of distrust after being cheated on."

You know what? It felt like, it almost felt like you get punked. It almost feels like somebody punkin' you. It's like, "Man, you can't even keep your woman from cheatin' on you. It's like what kind of dude are you? You ain't got no game." I mean, other cats would be like, "Man, if you was…" And then you know you hear people say, "You know what? If you was handlin' yo' business, it would've never happened." One thing I do know is that I never ever have control over another person. Now, her reasons for doing what she did could be totally different from what I think they were. All I know is, I felt disrespected and I felt powerless. I felt like a little punk who couldn't keep his woman, and that hurt. It would hurt for me to see her talk to another guy, even if he was just a friend. At times, it even hurt me to see her talk to some of her relatives. I always thought she was talking about me on the phone to other people. I always thought she was sneaking off to go be with this dude. I was driving myself crazy, literally, just wondering what she was doing. It was on my mind 24/7. I would make calls in the morning, at the time I was at home and she was in college. She was at school, and the guy she was cheating with was at the same school. So that situation alone just hurt. Like man, she's with dude right now. Every time I would think about her, I would think that she was with him. It had driven me to the point where we ended up breaking up. That even hurt more. I was like, "Man, not only did she cheat on me, now she wants to break up with me."

All those events, I think, had to happen because it hurt so badly, I didn't know what to do. At one point, I contemplated suicide. I'm like, well, I'll just jump in front of a bus and I'll make her hurt that way. I mean, it was no way I could think to hurt her other than if I was dead. Maybe then she'd cry, or maybe if I was dead, that would show her. But in doing all of that, it led me to getting saved. I mean, I had nowhere else to go at the time. I was homeless. Then we finally got into it and I had nowhere to stay.

Losing my girl, it felt like I was in a foreign land, in another state where I didn't have a lot of relatives. I literally cried out to the Lord at that point. Everything my mother taught me about the Lord, being saved, this is all you have to do. All of those tools she gave me just came to the forefront and I forgot about everything else. And I said, "You know what? I'll give it a shot." At that point, I cried out to God and at that very second I was saved. I mean, that relationship was actually a blessing in disguise. Even though it was painful, even though it hurt, I felt like it was worth it. I think just like when Christ died on the cross, all the things that happened to him had to happen. I think that, like him, all those things that happened to me had to happen for me to get saved because if they hadn't, I don't know if I would have or not.

I could remember it like yesterday. I mean, I remember the day I got saved. It was February 7, 1991 at three in the afternoon. I remember that specific time and day because of what was going on in my life... a lot of pain. I mean, I was just desolate. There was just nowhere to go. I didn't feel loved at all by that woman after us breaking up. Even though I accepted it, I just couldn't get her to be with me anymore. And even if I did, I wanted her to be on the same level spiritually. And at that point, I don't think I talked to another woman. After I got saved all I wanted was the word. I was more or less on fire at that time and I was trying to please God instead of a woman. I ended up moving back to California.

When I came back to California it was in 1993. That relationship lasted about two to three years. I came back in '93 and that's when I met my daughter's mother. I wasn't looking. I was about twenty-nine or thirty, and I wasn't looking for a woman. I was more or less going to church, trying to do the right thing. My attraction to her was… strangely, she reminded me of my ex. I was like, "She's kind of closed off. It's kind of a better situation because she's not my ex and she knows nothing about what I just went through and I can start anew with this woman." It felt good at first, but the attraction was more or less with me. It was spiritual. But it quickly became physical, even though we weren't involved in sex. It became a physical attraction because of her maturity level. She was really immature. I think she was about, seven or eight, years younger than me. I was like, man, "She's kind of silly. She's kind of goofy. She's just the kind of woman I need. If I need to manipulate her, it's in the bag. If I need her to do something for me, I won't get questioned." She was more or less easy to manipulate, easy to talk to. She wasn't materialistic. Like I said, I wasn't really looking for someone, but if I was, she would have been the perfect candidate. But in doing that, I ended up making more mistakes with her than with any other woman.

She got pregnant, but she also had a lot of other friends, so I questioned it. Yeah, male friends, so I questioned whether the child was mine or not, and that hurt her really bad, you know? And it didn't hurt me at all. It was a legitimate question, I thought. I ended up being with her for all the wrong reasons. We both were in the same church. Our families knew each other. We kind of grew up together, but got together later on in life. I think I stayed with her for the next twelve years without totally committing.

"Define your understanding of being in a relationship without a real commitment."

When I say not being totally committed, I mean she was not someone I wanted to marry. I knew that we wouldn't get married. I mean, I knew that she was someone I could walk away from and be okay. I felt pressured at times to be with her because she was pregnant. I felt pressure from the church. Everyone wanted us to do the right thing, and I wanted to do the right thing too. But for me, the right thing was to take care of the child. For me, the right thing wasn't to take her and marry her. It was like, "Man, I'm not in love with her." This was maybe the first time that I was with someone I wasn't in love with. It was really tough for me.

"Describe what it felt like being in a loveless relationship, just going through the motions."

To be honest, I was content with it. I felt contentment. I didn't feel like I was hurting her. I mean, had I been given ultimatums or had I been forced to make decisions, I think if she had been a stronger woman and said, "Look, this is what I want to do," or if she had asked me, "What are your plans for our lives?" meaning, her and this child, I would have given it more thought. I was really content with her not asking me about it. It never crossed my mind to say, "You know what? I think I'm in love with you," when I was not.

I more or less went through the motions with this woman. I did feel a big void. I felt like a lot was missing, not just a little bit. I felt like we didn't have anything in common other than the child. I tried to do right by God first. But I was like, "Lord, you know that I'm not happy." It took a lot of prayer for me to stay there. I was with other women because of that void. I met a lot of good women—women that were good for me. I felt like I was missing out on my soul mate. I felt like I was wasting her time. I had conversations with her, I don't know how many times, about how we should leave on good terms and I tried to convince her that it was "not for me but for you." I was sympathetic because I seen her being unhappy. I seen her wanting to do things, go out and dance and I saw how she had more fun with her friends than she had with me. I saw how she looked at other men and I also observed how she treated other men. Although I wasn't in love with her, I never disrespected her around other women. I had, I don't know, three or four different affairs while I was with her. I think one of which she knew about and that one affair I just really didn't care because I actually really cared about that other person. I had a lot in common with that person. That person really stimulated me emotionally, mentally and spiritually. That's where I needed to be in order to be in love. I've lusted after a lot of women, but only a few have stimulated me otherwise. I'm attracted to intelligence more than anything or I'm attracted to spiritual women. I stayed in that relationship twelve years and it just pissed me off. Even right now, until this day, I'm pissed off about it because like I said, I wasted her time, I wasted my time, and there was a child involved. I'm still pissed that I wasted so much time missing out on a healthy relationship.

Then your window gets smaller. As you get older, your window gets smaller and you say, "Man, I'm halfway there and I still haven't found someone to grow old with." I don't know. I was stuck between my daughter, such a beautiful little girl, that it was kind of like an anchor. I was anchored trying to stay there. I was never able to show her that I fully loved her mom, and I didn't think that was fair to her. We argued at times to where, I think my daughter felt like it was normal to see us argue about little things like leaving the light on or just stupid stuff. I wanted to show her a healthy relationship and I tried to do that and it made me miserable. I mean, I tried to show her that I loved her mom, even though I didn't. There was no kiss before you leave and no kiss when you came home. There was no "hello" or "good-bye." There was only complaints. "You been here all day and you have not done this or that." And I'm like, "Okay, how are you too?" I mean, it was miserable for both of us. I was more or less trying to be a peacemaker and I would just ignore the arguments a lot of time. I would try to find "outs" like going to the gym, going to play ball, anything to stay away from home. I knew that that's not someone I was in love with. If it were, it would have been just the opposite.

I mean, it seems that all of my relationships have been with the same woman with a different face. Then I had to question myself that maybe it's not them; maybe it's me and my choice of women. So, all of this time these relationships are all going bad. Could it have been my fault as well? If they're all ending up the same, then maybe I need to change my way of thinking.

"Why do you believe you sought out this type of woman?"

Why I picked this kind of woman? I don't know if it's for the same reason or different reasons. I know that all the women I have been in relationships with have been younger than me, not saying that they couldn't be mature enough to be in a relationship. I don't want to stereotype. But they have all been women who haven't graduated from college, women who have been in dysfunctional families like mine, and women that I'm more or less comfortable being around, knowing that they could relate to my background. I've stayed away from successful women, from sophisticated women, women that you look at and say, "I know she got a man" or women that you look at and think, "You know, she might be a little too strong for me, or she may just be a little too independent for me or maybe just she's not a good fit for me."

I don't know why I picked those types of women, but I know that I haven't picked a woman that's a challenge to me. I'm not sure why, but I do know that a lot of times when I look at a woman, I have to ask myself *what is the attraction*? I mean, sometimes it's one thing that you like. I mean, it could be her ears or her eyes. It could be just her smile. It could be one or several things about a woman that will keep you there. I mean, I could make a list of things that I like my woman to be like and I could say, "You know what? I'm not stopping at nothing less than this." And people would think I was crazy. But in order for me to have a healthy, successful, or longevity in a relationship, I would have to have a woman who I would be happy to see every day, a woman I was attracted to emotionally and physically. In the physical sense, I think as I have gotten older, it doesn't matter if she looks like a coke bottle. That's more or less a young man's thing. But I also won't just settle for any type of woman. I mean, I more or less like a woman I can talk to, communicate with. I don't know. I mean, it's not just one thing.

"You appear to be in deep reflection at this very moment, am I right?"

Well, just thinking about how I need to back track to when I was about nineteen or twenty. There was a young woman I grew up with in the neighborhood. I knew she liked me and I liked her too, but we never told each other that. We just kind of hooked up at times. Yes, we hooked up. I think it was more or less the drinking that would get us together. She's a really nice girl. Anyways, her mother was white and her dad was black. Her mom, I think more or less had issues with men. She didn't like men at all. There were some brothers in her life that had done her wrong, and maybe that's the reason. Her mom, all of a sudden, did not like me at all. She didn't want me coming around. She wouldn't let me come in the house. If I called, she would be real short on the phone. Fifteen years ago I ran into her [daughter]. I hadn't seen her in ten years. We went to this bar and sat down and started talking. She looked into my eyes and stated, "You know why my mom really doesn't like you?"

I was like, "Why?"

And she said, "Do you remember when I was house sitting at my friend's house and you came over?"

I said, "Yeah, I remember."

"Well, I got pregnant."

I said, "Really?"

"Yeah and my mom made me abort."

I never knew that. I mean, fifteen years later this is disclosed to me. I really liked her and she really liked me and I never knew she was pregnant. It brought tears to my eyes. I was hurt. I mean, until this day, I think about it and it hurts me because I even told her, "If I would have known that, today my life would be totally different right now. If I only had known then, we would have been together until this day." We both cried. Her mom kept her away from me from that day forth. That was an event that really hurt me too. I had no idea that she was pregnant. That was the first time I'd ever had sex. I was her first and she was mine. And when she told me that, it ripped my heart out to know that happened. So, I still live with that until this day. We're still friends. I don't see her much. Well, actually I don't see her at all. If I wanted to I could. She's still around, but you know her life went one way and mine went another. But if I had known that she was carrying my child, I think things would have been totally different. I think I would have been doing different things. I think I might not have even gone to jail. That had an effect on me. It continues to have a deep impact on my life. It impacted me, but it did not impact how I feel about women today because we were never boyfriend and girlfriend. She was more or less the girl next door. I really liked her and she really liked me. It could have potentially been a really good thing.

After everything I've been through in life, and all my teachings and lessons in love and being in relationships, my ability to love today is, I guess, impacted by all of those dynamics, especially not being able to commit and being afraid to commit. Yes, I'm afraid to commit. I'm afraid that the same thing will happen; the dysfunctional cycle will repeat itself.

I think that watching my mother's and father's relationships fail, watching my sister get divorced and remarried three times, watching my other sister get divorced (one of my sisters got beat half to death and lost her baby behind that relationship) and just seeing a lot of my friends be in unhealthy relationships, has made me fearful of marriage.

Even though I have difficulty with it, I think I'm stronger today than I was in the past. I think I'm getting there. It's still hard for me to say that I'm in love. I know I'm able to love, and I know that I have the capacity to love and I really, really do want to be in a relationship where I can be in love and know how it feels to be in love. However, at times, I don't think I actually know how to be in love because of so many failed relationships. Just seeing a lot of failed relationships has made me fearful. Don't get me wrong. I've seen people be together for sixty-seven years. My grandparents were together for sixty-something years. They were each other's first love. I think a lot of the stuff that goes on today— a lot of liberal things that go on today—have a lot to do with it. I think that our society has a negative view on relationships. I don't think people take relationships seriously. I think I've been in a lot of relationships that I didn't take serious because I wasn't with a person that was serious enough to say they loved me. I've always had issues telling somebody I loved them.

You know, I love my mother to death. I love her. She is the nicest person I know. I'd do anything for her, but she didn't always say "I love you." I think about that and I'm like, "she loved everybody," and I think it's just expected. You just expect her to love you anyway, whether she says it or not. If more people would have told me I love you when I was growing up, it would be much easier for me to express it. At times I ask myself, "What is love? How can I get it?" I really didn't know how to love anyone until I got saved, until God showed me how much He loved me. I was like, "Wow, now maybe I can love someone." Then my whole thinking about relationships started off with the spiritual aspect. I try to be in love. Even recently, I can say I was in love but not able to show it.

"What's keeping you from expressing love?"

That's a good question. I think when I'm in a relationship, I just kind of expect that person to know I love them. I feel like at times, I shouldn't have to tell you that because you should know because I'm here for you, because I would do anything for you, because we spend a lot of time together. It's not hard for me to show it. It's hard for me to say it. Then it is hard for me to show it at times. I don't know how to describe the act of me showing someone that I love them. I guess I could express it, but most of the times my actions don't show it. I've always had a problem with that.

At this stage in the game, with women my age, most of them have been through the ringer. I love the fact that women are so strong. I know that most women are a lot stronger than men, and a lot of men won't admit that. I believe that women can take a lot emotionally. I know that many women cry silently, but I also know they take more than a man could take. I've seen women get dogged. I mean, I'm actually responsible for some of that and it hurts me to know that I am, because I think back and I'm like, "Man, I was not a good boyfriend at all. Even though I was there, it's like, "Man, I could have did more. I could have at least loved her enough to say, "It's not working. We need to chill." And I usually wait for the woman to say that. I find myself not being strong enough to say, "This is all I want from you." You know, "I don't think we're going to be able to move on beyond this point." I mean, even now, and I thought to myself that I was a good enough man or a strong enough man to say, "Hey, look, I would love to be with you and to start a life with you," and I'm not able to do that at times. I'm not able to say, "Look, this is what I need from you and this is what I want. Are you cool with that? We can take it from there." Instead, I tend to get into relationships where I'm friends first, and it's not intentional, but it just eases into something else. It's like you get into a relationship and you're talking about this and you're talking about that. You're talking about your family, and all of a sudden you're talking a lot. You know what I'm saying? Then it's like, "Instead of doing all of this talking, why don't we go hook up and go eat?" Then you ease in, and all of a sudden you find yourself enjoying that person's company and one day turns into another and you're looking at them differently. It doesn't take alcohol to do that. You could just look at someone and you know whether you have feelings for them or not. I've met some wonderful women that I would love to be with, and end up hurting them bad. I didn't realize it. It's like I didn't mean to do that and I'm really sorry. You know, and then if I see them with somebody else, and they're just as happy as they can be. I sit back and I'm like, "Man, that could be me." But then I'm also saying, "Well, why can't it be with you?"

I think everybody deserves to be happy at some point. I don't know if I'm the type that's going to be single forever or the type of person who can't find someone that he's good enough for. I don't want to say there's no one good enough for me. A lot of times I wonder if I'm good enough for her. Can I provide for what she needs?

In the current relationship I find myself having what the other person wants. It's like, "I already got that. I already have that. I already have been through that." It's not fair to someone else to say because I've already had it, I can't give that to you because I've already done it. But it also hurts to say, "You know what? Since I feel that way, it might be best for you to move on and find someone who can give you what you need." Because like I said, the window has gotten really small, and life is really short and you know, I'm finding that out. Before I start to love anyone, I have to make sure that's what I want to do.

"Do you have the capacity to love deeply?"

At this present time, I think I do have the capacity to love deeply. Because I've matured I don't have anything to lose if I do, because I deserve it, and someone else does too. I don't know how it feels to love deeply because I've always had reservations when I've loved. I've thought, *hey, it may not work out so maybe I shouldn't put my all into it*. I think now I do because I don't have anything to lose.

I don't have anything to prove. My boys aren't going to talk about me if I do. I think I do have the capacity to love deeply. *How deep?* is the question. I can probably love a person as much as they love me. I mean, as much as I can give, I can probably do it.

"This is simply your opinion. Can a man love as deeply as a woman?"

I haven't been able to. I'm not sure if a man can. I'm not sure if a man has that characteristic to love as deep as a woman. I think a woman complements a man. I think a man would have to learn how to love deeply through a woman. Or if he was going to love as much as she can, he'd have to learn from her. That's a tough question. I mean, because women love hard. They love hard even when we don't know they do. I think that if a man was to love as deeply as a woman, he would definitely have to learn how to do it from the woman who loves him deeply.

When it's all said and done, and you've been through relationships and you've grown and you've come to a place where you want to love, I think that most women who have been through a lot will be willing to give a man a chance. I think it just starts with that. I don't think finding the right person means to give everyone a chance. But if you are interested in a man, if you are attracted to man, make sure that the attraction is not all that you're going to trust.

It's hard to say, because I still want a chance. Even though I've been in unhealthy relationships and even though I've broken a few hearts, I still want my chance. I think that if women would give us a chance to learn, I mean, for me I try to learn from a woman, you know, what she likes, what she dislikes. I try to pay attention to her and listen to her. I try to keep it real simple. I've never been a complicated guy, except when it comes to showing love and emotions. I mean, I have issues in that area. Other than that, I think men are real simple. I think we're real easy. We don't require a lot. I think most women require more attention and I think they just want the attention to come from their man. I think if they don't get it, they'll get it from another man. I don't think any woman should give up on love because of what they've been through. It's just hard to see women go through what they go through looking for that. I mean, I can't say I've really been looking for love out there, because I've been in a few long-term relationships.

I feel like I've missed out on a lot. I've gotten to the point where I've almost wanted to just give up or just go with the flow. You know, whatever comes along, and that's what I've been used to. I think that's what women have to stop doing is settling for whatever comes along. Just because a guy smiles at them, tells them they're pretty, or spends a few dollars on them; you can't be naive. You more or less have to trust your heart and pay attention to warning signs. There's no way to evaluate a man right away or assess a woman right away. You just more or less have to follow your instincts and your life experiences. I mean, if I had to give a woman advice about not giving up on a man, it would be to just not give up on them. It's just hard to say.

For me, I mean, I've always had issues. I don't think I've ever been the type to approach a woman with no game. I've always thought I had a lil' bit, but I've never had to use it. I've always been low key, more or less genuine most of the time, not trying to sound like I got the magic touch or nothing. Most of the time I've been approached and I've never had to use my game. So, I'm real rusty in that area. I've always either met someone through someone or just from seeing them on a daily basis. I was recently seeing someone and how she and I hooked up is that I used to see her on a daily basis and found out we had a lot in common. I think that's more or less what a woman has to do; just find someone that they have a lot in common with. You know, they can go to the websites like eHarmony and Match.com. You can try it out, but there's no way to tell if you're compatible with someone unless you be with them. You know, just like everything, every relationship is going to change. You know you got your "honeymoon period" and I think that's what has kept me from committing. I want every day of my relationship to be new. I want everything to just always be good. And to me, that's not a good thing because time goes by and you leave the other person hanging, and they're like, "Why can't you love me like I love you? Or "Why can't you commit to me like I'm willing to commit to you?" A lot of times my answer is, "I like things the way they are," or "I don't want us to be like my past relationships. I want it to be like we just met. I want our every day to be like our first day. I don't want to lose that feeling." I think that keeps me from going further; I want it to stay brand-new. I want it to always be new. I want that first kiss to always feel the same. I don't know if I'm trying the same thing, expecting a different result, but I think it's good and bad for me. It's good for me, but maybe that's my selfishness. You know, always wanting it to be good for me, but leaving her hanging and before you know it, a day, a month, a couple years will go by. You know time flies when you're having fun. That's what I was telling my friend. I was like, "You know what? We must be having fun because time is going by really fast." Like I said, I've met maybe two women—

three at the most— that I could probably be with for the rest of my life. And they have been wonderful.

I just don't want love to be lost. I mean, I know I can love, but like I said, we just all have to be retro lovers because today love means a whole lot of different things than what it used to. Love to some means that if I smack you down and go to jail, then you come bail me out. That's kind of extreme, but that's what love means in some cases. I think love was just lost way back in time. I think women need to go back to the old-fashioned cats, the kind that would open your door, and not call you names when you get mad, pay all your bills, and feel that it's his duty to provide for you on every level. That's what I'm talking about.

"I must say that it has been a pleasure. I appreciate your honesty."

It was good for me to go back and face some wounds that had not completely healed.

Letting Go

Have you ever needed assistance with an issue but refused to reach out to HIM because you knew that by doing so, you would be forced to confront your behavior and emotions and perhaps you weren't ready to fully let go? You were not ready to fully let go and let GOD.

It takes LOVE, FAITH and COURAGE to stand on the front line and confront your deepest fears because facing one's reality can be traumatic. It can be traumatizing because in doing so, a shift may be needed; a shift in your actions and in your thoughts. COURAGE is about letting go and FAITH is about trusting that GOD will do what it is HE does best.

HE can heal your heart and give you a peace that's beyond anything you ever imagined.

~Mary E. Gilder

Drake

CHAPTER FOUR
High Cheat Potential

Zodiac Sign: Aries
Approximate Age: Thirties
Occupation: Ph.D. Business Administration
Passions: Mentoring
Hobbies: Traveling and Biking

"I think, at the time, I was developing a very strong sense of "me." I felt very comfortable with my identity I was developing, so I knew what I could offer. I knew I wanted to care for somebody else. I knew that I had a lot of love that I wanted to share. I wanted to communicate and I wanted to be intimate. I knew that none of that would come from this relationship. So I think, secretly, I began to cultivate these connections either through my friends, through other people and through my work. A good friend told me, "You

have a high cheat potential, and partly because you're with the wrong person." —Drayke

"How were you raised to treat a woman?"

How was I raised to treat women? That's question one? (Laughter) I think from very early on, I guess, my understanding of how to treat a woman came from the things I saw my father do, the things my mother accepted from my father. So, I must begin by stating that my dad was a very good role model of that. My dad was your typical patriarch in the sense that he had a very clear vision of where he wanted to be with his family. Some of the expectations he had for us were for us to work hard and to eventually establish families of our own. But more importantly, he always said that if we were to pursue a significant other, she should share the same values that we do and that she should work hard or be willing to contribute to our mutual goals.

My dad didn't really say much beyond that, but he modeled, I think, good behavior. He and I see it now in my current relationships, how I am. I'm very much like my dad. He uses a lot of humor and he's relatively lighthearted when it comes to my mom. So, I guess growing up, I saw my parents crack jokes on each other and they would laugh a lot. Sometimes Dad would be upset and he would be stern and firm as well, but I think he always respected my mom. He had a basic respect for her as an individual. I think my dad recognized that they were both individual beings that were growing, of course separately, because everyone is on their own journey in life. So, I guess what I learned from my dad is just a mutual respect for who people are and where they are and not judging them because they don't match some stereotype in our head of a good woman. I guess what I got is "As long as she works hard, you have shared values and you both reciprocate a common respect, you will be moving in a good direction." That's kind of what he showed us and modeled for us in his marriage.

My mom, on the other hand, also helped me to form my ideologies and expectations as a man. My mom was extremely loyal and extremely devoted. She encouraged us to dream. I think she was a little more creative, so some of her ambitions in life kind of challenged my dad a little bit because he is such a straight and narrow guy. He enjoyed seeing my mom open businesses and stuff like that, though. Mom was the kind of woman who was extremely ambitious. She challenged the notion that while it's very difficult, as a woman you can have a family, you can go to school, you can achieve. You might not proceed at the pace you'd like, but it's possible if you devote yourself to it. Mom always asked that we respect women and treat them as our equal. She also said, "A man that doesn't share his feelings is not really a man. And that it takes more courage to be vulnerable and to share your emotions than to hold them in." So, she always encouraged that we express ourselves and that we feel and remain in touch with our feelings and make sure we communicated those things. In terms of her requests of us as young men in the dating field, she wanted us to be responsible and respectful. She stressed that women were creatures to be admired, adorned and cared for, and that all men should treat them with respect. She was also very adamant that if you were to create a child, it would be your responsibility as a man to make sure that you took care of your kids. What else? I'm just going back in time with things I remember hearing: take care of your responsibilities, you respect somebody, you respect their word and you try not to judge them.

"Describe your first experience with love."

My first experience with love, or at least my first attempt to understand what love meant or to develop a belief about what love should be, I think really began when I was about sixteen. I began dating a young lady named Karla, who I met in a grocery store, Kroger's to be exact. I saw her and I think I immediately was attracted to her. There was something about her that stood out and just appeared very different from the other young ladies I knew at the time. So, I began what you would call "courting" her. I was old school in my ways. So, it began with invitations for small bites to eat because we both worked in the grocery store. I made my way up to asking her to go to the movies and she told me no at first, which was kind of cool to be challenged. Eventually, we did go to the movies and started spending a lot of time together. I think ultimately it almost seemed like a friendship at the time. What I guess I didn't realize in my friendship is that I was almost mirroring what I thought I saw my parents doing. I tried to just be as much of my dad as possible because I thought that's how you show love. By that I mean that I would take care of all of the financial responsibilities. I made sure that we spent quality time together and I tried to make her feel special.

I remember one Thanksgiving, she had to work for the holiday, so I got a five-dollar chicken and I went into the break room and I set up a candlelight dinner in the super market for Thanksgiving dinner. That went over really well. I think that relationship persisted over time as my "first relationship." I mean, you're trying to understand love and I remember calling all of my old cousins and trying to understand these new feelings I was having. For example, I went from "head over heels," where I would use the butterflies in my stomach as an indicator that I loved her and my excitement at that time as an indicator of love. I think I hit a crossroads at one point in time when those things kind of stopped occurring, and I guess that's really where I started asking myself the question: "Does this mean I don't love her anymore?" I was under the impression that the butterflies should always be there, so I think for a period of about two years I was grappling with an understanding of "How do you love somebody, but not feel intensely all the time?" So, I thought because I didn't feel so intensely, that maybe I loved her but maybe I didn't. It was a very difficult space for me to be in. I began seeking out literature. I read a bell hooks book, "*All About Love*," just trying to really tap into an understanding of what love was as an expression. What did it look like? What was my version and definition of love? What was the kind of love I needed? I think over time what I realized was everyone has the capacity to be loved, but I think how we need to be loved can be very different. It doesn't make it any less significant, just that it's different. So I'd say from about 18 to 20, I was really maybe just kind of coming to terms with what that meant.

At the same time, I think we both graduated high school and we both enrolled in a community college in Texas. There were a lot of tough questions before us. Where are we going? What is this relationship about? At the time, I was convinced that I needed to go to college if I wanted to get out of Texas. I think at that time we started growing a part. I wanted to move to a faraway place. She kind of wanted to stay there and that put the relationship on the rocks a little bit. Not to draw a contrast, but I started noticing that what I wanted out of life was a little bit different than what she wanted. I had a lot of adults back then telling me "You're about to embark upon the greatest journey of change and that's your twenties. It's idealistic to think that you guys are going to get married and get together. But you know you're going to change who you are, fundamentally as a person, the things you need, etcetera." I didn't really believe them so I just escalated my commitment to her saying, "No, it's going to work out la la la," but I think ultimately she went away to school and I went away to school and I think things began to change. Our experiences apart gave us an opportunity to learn more about whom we were, and who we were becoming, and I think our differences and experiences allowed us to have a healthy conversation. But,

I think the conversations were still very different in terms of the directions they were headed.

From about 20 to 22, she had gone to a couple different colleges, maybe three to four different colleges. I guess she was finding herself, and one way to do that was through going to different colleges. I left Texas and went to Atlanta to attend College. That was a decision I made. So, about a year into my undergrad, she decided that she was going to go to a college close by. Her rationale for that was she'd be able to get out of school sooner and graduate and get on her feet. So, a year later, she moved down. I was very much against it. I felt that these were our times to grow and have our experiences and if we were to come back together that would not be the case. I felt and still believe that she came there with the intent of making the relationship work and I think that the distance, for her, made her feel very insecure. I think she masked the insecurity by saying how these things would contribute to the future she was going to have. And because I was so future-oriented, trying to figure out what I wanted to do with myself, these things sounded attractive and made sense.

She came down and I said, "Look, you got to get yourself together. I have two roommates, and it's probably not a good idea for you to stay with me. I really don't believe in living with anyone that I'm not married to."

And she said, "I'll stay six weeks, and then I'll find my own apartment." Well, six weeks became six months and I think at that time our relationship started to experience a big decline. I was very involved, I had a lot of friends, and I had a lot of things going on as far as student government. I think, to some extent, she didn't like that I was involved so much, and a lot of the things I was doing became questioned. I was pledging a fraternity at the time and she said that she wouldn't be with me if I pledged because she didn't agree with it. I felt like I was in my space of growing, but I had to balance the expectations someone else had on me. In my mind, based on what I saw my parents do and the mistakes they made along the way, it seemed they supported each other whether they agreed with it or not. So, I guess my expectation was, "This is something that's important to me and I'm of the mind that you, as my partner, should be supportive of this. I think that was again another pivotal moment where I really asked myself *"Is this something healthy for me?"*

Recognizing from my past how significant support was, or at least seeing in my parents' relationship, I had to ask myself, *"Is this something healthy for me? Is this a good relationship?"* Things kind of moved on. She remained and the relationship continued to be rocky. I was contemplating graduate school at the time and even though she was behind me as far as, graduating, she was still thinking about graduate school too. Then in the fall of 2001, which was about two years after I was in my undergrad, she became pregnant. Then our son Tyler was born in July 2002.

Having Tyler was a big turning point for me, because I was a little naïve about how the world worked. I just wanted to graduate and backpack around Asia. I just wanted to be a free spirit and figure life out when I got around 30. I know, very idealistic, not realistic at all. I feel like having Tyler made me more mature and it leveled me out a little bit more. I had to consider how I was going to take care of his well-being, while at the same time making sure that I grew.

The expectations she had of me when she told me about my son were not realistic and I remember telling her just that. I couldn't believe it. I felt like I had a lot of opportunities ahead and at that time I felt like the walls were closing in on me, in the sense that I would have to forgo a lot of the opportunities I had spent a couple years trying to create. I think for her, and for me, the expectation was that I had to stop living, get a job, get married and do the happily-ever-after thing. I was raised that you take care of your child, so that, I understood. Actually, I went so far as to even purchase an engagement ring. I was of the belief that it was my responsibility. I'd been with this young lady for "XYZ" amount of time, and things may be difficult, but sometimes you have to handle your responsibilities. So, I decided to give her a ring with the purpose of becoming engaged and moving forward as married individuals.

I felt like because I was such a free spirit, it made people feel uncomfortable. To me, people just wanted to clip my wings; that's the best description of it. All of her family, and others, were all like, "Oh now, Drayke, you can't travel anymore. You can't do this. You can't do that."

I had a conversation with my mom and my dad and I said, "Look, everybody wants me to just work and not follow my goals."

I was having a very tough time dealing with the expectations, and they said, "Well, you know other people's views of love are that you have to sacrifice when you have a child." My parents were like, "Your children live around you; you have to keep learning and growing and pushing forward because they're going to learn from all of that. Don't stop living because you have a child. You live more because you have one so that they can see the world as well."

Karla's family was a little more old school. They thought, "You just have to settle down." It was a very challenging time for me. In fact, in 2001, when I found out she was pregnant, I went on a trip to Morocco that December because everyone told me, "You're not going to be able to travel anymore; it's irresponsible." So, I think purposefully, I scheduled a trip. I went to Morocco and Spain and Portugal, and backpacked with seven of my friends for about thirteen days. I took a hiatus to take perspective on what I wanted to do. For me, it was a difficult internal challenge, because I had been raised that you take care of your responsibilities. So, part of me was going to go ahead and get the job and get married and just suck it up, even though I knew the relationship wasn't there. Even though I knew, I think I had a jaded view of what love meant. I also had an understanding that there was a child to consider. People think that children can fill the gaps where the relationship left off. And I think, for me, I kind of [fell into the same thinking]. A couple of arguments later, along with me travelling, I became defiant, just very defiant. I started working more. I said that I was going to graduate school. I felt like I had invested a lot in undergrad, and it would be foolish to just be a police officer as my dad was. He was pressuring me. It was a tough time. But then I decided, "Look, I got to be true to myself. Graduate school is something I want to do, so I'm going to do it."

And Karla, at the time, disagreed with it. She was like, "We should be in graduate school together. We have to do this together. We need to work together and take our time." But I think at that point, I started developing a small resentment toward her, because during the time Tyler was born my anxiety elevated. I was about to leave and I was becoming frustrated with our situation. It had taken her about seven years to finish her bachelor's degree. She was in about five or six different schools; she was just everywhere. I felt like the only way to move my family ahead was if I started doing my work and being the breadwinner. I kind of adopted the mindset that I was going to have to make the decisions. I was going to have to find a job. I had envisioned a partnership and when I realized it wasn't a partnership anymore, I became resentful. It was almost as if I had to figure out a way to take care of a child and another adult, and it didn't sit well with me. I knew then that what we had couldn't be love, and I kind of grappled with the idea that I was settling. I felt like a part of me was dying. I knew a part of me had died, because I knew that I tried to make the other parts live. I tried to travel more; I threw myself into my work and into my child. A lot of these things were justifications to fill, I think, a void. I was longing for an emotional connection to a person and I think I made a connection to a person by being cognitive. When I say that, I mean I had to think about how to make the relationship work, rather than feel that it was going to work, if that makes sense. The feeling partly came after I realized that I had to be very rational and do what made sense. I believed that I could push forward, get a career and that I could still maintain my autonomy. But these were all based on external achievements, interactions with other people, and essentially I envisioned me just working all of the time and never being home because of the emotional black hole that existed in the relationship. I challenged her to go to counseling because she wasn't very emotional herself. She couldn't really open up for whatever reasons. But, as for me, I felt empty. I had always longed for a connection and I was very optimistic that one existed. I don't think I believed in soul mates, but I think I believed that you can strike enough of an emotional balance that you can feel relatively complete with someone. That doesn't mean that you came to the relationship empty, but it means that for the days when you're not strong, the other person can be strong for you and vice versa.

I think at the time I was developing a very strong sense of me. I felt very comfortable with the identity I was developing, so I knew what I could offer. I knew how I wanted to care for somebody else. I knew that I had a lot of love that I wanted to share. I wanted to communicate and I wanted to be intimate. I knew that none of that would come from this relationship. So I think secretly I began to cultivate connections either through my friends, through other people or through my work. A good friend told me, "You have a high cheat potential and partly because you're with the wrong person."

"Very interesting, Drayke. Please expand on what was perceived as your high cheat potential."

I think my understanding of relations, sexual relations, is that's a space where two souls commune. They come together, they share and interact. I personally believe God is very present in that moment. I think that can only exist when there is true and sincere caring, and concern and love for the other person. I think when those things aren't present, it just becomes sex. It's not an act of making love, and I think a lot of times for whatever reason, there is a deficient connection. I believe that sometimes sex becomes the filler for the void in other areas. It's just purely tactile and physical. You don't connect with the person. You don't feel open with them. It's simply like engaging in the act because, well, this is all I have left to do. It is the one area where you can salvage something. That might sound really bad, but I don't know. It's not that you view the person as an object, but that place where you guys could connect in the middle is just not there. It seems like an act, if you will. Your potential to cheat increases if you seek out another to fill that void and there was definitely a void.

"Did feelings of empathy, sympathy or compassion cease to exist in your relationship?"

I think observing her care for my son made me empathetic and more compassionate toward her because I saw her nursing and taking care of Tyler. I felt very good about that. I felt that it was my responsibility to take care and provide a space where that could always occur. So, I felt closer to her, in some regard, in large part because I grew up in a two-parent home, so seeing this and being part of it was not far off from how I grew up. So, it felt very natural because that's what I had always seen, despite our inability to connect.

"When did you come to understand that there was a significant shift?"

When did I come to the realization? I think the biggest shift occurred after Tyler was born. We had Tyler in my junior year of undergrad and I think the shift came when I decided I wanted to go to graduate school. She hadn't finished her degree yet. She didn't know what she wanted to do, but I told her I wanted to do this advanced degree thing and I think it was threatening for her. I applied everywhere. I applied for a special position at NYU. I had New York City police jobs, pharmaceutical sales jobs. I got accepted into two grad programs. I recall her telling me how selfish I was and that I wasn't considering her. She also stated that we were supposed to work together, go to school at the same time and share in the responsibility of raising Tyler. It was essentially what she wanted. And for me, I really didn't see the world with those glasses. I just feel that you can't do everything at the same time. Somebody has got to step up sometime and somebody else steps back. You kind of do this dance. She never had any strong models in her home. Her parents were divorced. I just felt like she was being very unrealistic. I think when the acceptances started coming in; it became a very big point of contention for her. I remember having these discussions, when I was in Atlanta and she had returned to Texas for a semester. Upon hearing that I was going to graduate school, she moved back down to Texas with my son again. Now mind you, my son in a very short time lived in Texas twice and Atlanta twice. She didn't have a plan. She got an apartment, incurred all this debt and you know she kept telling me about how she was going try to get into school and all this…I think she was just giving me a lot of lip service, telling me the things I wanted to hear so that I would just continue to deal with her. I think when I told her I was going to school and the places I was thinking of going, I think she got really scared.

At that point, the only control she really had over me and over the situation and my decisions was by using Tyler. I recall very explicitly being out and about at eleven o'clock at night and she was like, "Oh, Tyler needs Pampers." *You just realized he needed those at eleven?* She would kind of do this Tyler-needs thing, or my-car-is-broken-down thing, or I-have-no-money," thing, knowing that my values were you're supposed to take care of your responsibility. I think she understood that and was playing me. That lasted for a little while. I felt bad for her. I just kept continuing to do, and just tried to help her get on her feet with Tyler, etcetera. I think it took me about two or three years to realize I was being played. So, for me, I think it made me more resentful toward her, but I didn't really know how to be there for Tyler without being there for her. I think she coupled her and Tyler together all of the time. I would be very clear in saying "Look, this is a problem that doesn't involve Tyler. This involves us."

But she'd be like, "Oh, how are you going to do that to me and Tyler?"

I felt like her tools at the time were to make me feel guilty by painting a picture that my child was struggling and that the struggle was a direct result of me being selfish. And me being selfish was attributed to me wanting to go to grad school and be away from her. I was very unhappy. I felt horrible. I felt incredibly guilty. I felt abused because my guilt was being played on all the time. I wasn't mature enough then to see it for what it was. But you know, first-time parent, I'm young, I'm in my early twenties, and I'm just trying to gain an understanding of the world for me, let alone understand it for me and my son and my son's mother. It was a very challenging time.

I decided to push forward with the school thing. I tell you, I was in California maybe a year and a half, and she came to California to try and salvage the relationship and get back together. Then the next thing you know, she wants to come out to California because "I can get a job there; it's easier employment. I can't get anything here. You know we're living in the ghetto." She said all of this stuff to make me feel bad. I was like, "Look, I don't agree with your decision; however, it's your decision, and if you think this is best for you and where you're going, then I'll support. I had this same conversation before she came down to Atlanta. But this time I felt like it was a deliberate encroachment on what I was trying to do. I think in her head, maybe she was trying to make me have a better relationship with Tyler. I don't know what her motivation was. I know that her coming here [to California] was incredibly stressful.

"How so? Describe to me what the situation was like."

I felt anxious and scared. I felt like I lacked control. I felt like she was going to come here and I was going to have to take care of her because she didn't have the resources to survive. All of these things rang true. She came here with $3,000, and she said she had a job, but it took a few weeks for that to materialize. It was just bad. I told her she could stay with me for three days (because I remembered my situation in Atlanta where she wound up staying for six months). On the fifth day I had to kick her out. That was a bad feeling. I had to say, "You have to leave my house otherwise I'm going to call the police. For five days all she would do was lay down all day saying how tired she was, how she was trying to get it together, but couldn't do it by herself, etc. My thing was this, I didn't really care. You don't get a lot of excuses in life. I lacked compassion for her because everything for her was an excuse. Here it is, I was trying to be at my prime and she was here to interfere by becoming dependent and saying, "I can't do it." I think she was playing on me because she knew I would step up all of the time.

"How did this make you feel?"

I felt used, angry and frustrated. I felt scared that I wasn't going to finish my program. I really just felt sad for Tyler as I cycled through all of those emotions.

"Were you her only target? Did her apparent dysfunctions reach beyond you?"

Oh man, Mary, yes. There were times when she was very extreme with people. I was trying to start a relationship with a beautiful young lady and Karla went ballistic. I can think of probably four people off hand this occurred with. One time when I was down in Atlanta as an undergrad, she came to visit me before she decided to move there. She went through all of my emails, and decided to write letters about me to the people in my email. She told them that I was not interested in them because I had a girl. I was living with my cousin at the time, and he said, "Look, if a person can't respect your personal space, you probably do not need to be with them." And I kind of gave her the benefit of the doubt. I said, "Well, maybe she's insecure."

After that, I started chatting with a close female friend and we were maintaining communication through email. Karla started emailing my friend as if she were some third-party person that knew both of us mutually and she was sending all of these bad messages to my friend. She even called my friend and left messages on her machine. It was very crazy. So I confronted Karla about that and as a consequence, rightfully my friend became frustrated, so that dissolved that. I confronted her and she claimed that she was going to kill herself and that she couldn't take it and that I needed to get to Texas. Just all types of...I'm sorry. This experience with Karla was psychological abuse and I buried a lot of this pain and now it's coming to the surface.

"As we sit and discuss your past, it does appear that old wounds are resurfacing."

Yeah, they absolutely are. I can still recall the time when she stated that she was going to kill herself. She stated that she wouldn't be alive tomorrow. Just all types of crazy stuff is resurfacing. After one of these episodes, I started to figure out that every person I would try to have a relationship with, her same methods of sabotage would occur. Each relationship was very different; however, the only common denominator was Karla. So, it was the first time I had to look at this person who I thought really cared about my well-being as potentially having a very secret motive to win by all costs. She wanted to win by default. She had some issues. I told my mom, I promise you, Mary, maybe like in 2005, I said, "Mom, if I come up missing, this might be a stretch, but if something ever happens to me, please check Karla first." I was getting really scared. I thought maybe she might try to poison me or something, because of the things she would do. And then she would lie and deny them completely. When I figured it out and told her, "Look, I'm leaving you," she was all, "Oh, I'm going to hurt myself, and your son is not going to have a parent." Mary, it was crazy. It was absolutely crazy. Phew!

"At some point did you feel that perhaps you were dealing with maladaptive behavior?"

Editor's note: Maladaptive behavior refers to types of behaviors that inhibit a person's ability to adjust to particular situations. This type of behavior is often used to reduce one's anxiety, but the result is dysfunctional and non-productive.

I was nonjudgmental. I just kind of thought, *this is my responsibility and this is where she is. I need to at least be here to help her get on her feet.* I just really tried to see the positives for what they were and just tried to say, "She's just in a bad space right now." And I tried to be forgiving and caring and really see the better part of her. I think for a long time it kept me blinded. It kept me from seeing her for who she really was, which for me she was someone who was either very depressed, had some childhood wounds that hadn't been dealt with, or something clinical because the relationship was very, very sick.

She came to California, and I think my biggest realization was last year when she arrived. Before she moved here, I started dating a young lady and Karla started leaving voicemails on the young lady's phone. She was calling and saying, "You're trying to break up my home," etcetera, etcetera. And that's kind of where it began. Her friends started calling the young lady and then she went so far as to call me on my phone as if she were the young lady I was dating. She would pretend to be her in the background like, "Oh, I don't know why he's with me, but I'm just using him." She would send me text messages, because there's a way through the phone where you can see a text message but change the number where it's coming from. She would send me messages as if she were the young lady I was dating. Her strategy has always been to put doubt in the people I'm dealing with. So by default she could come to the rescue and pretend to be the most stable person I've had. But, uh you know, the gig was up. I actually, during that time, had finally figured out what was going on. I completely ignored her. I cut her off. She would write me letters and come by my house at all hours in the night. I had to get a restraining order against her.

Um, one time, I was going to work and as soon as I opened my door, she jumped into the car and wouldn't get out. I wound up going to work late; I had to call the cops. The cops had to tell her to get out of the car and to leave me alone. I had my tires cut. I believe that was her, but I'm not sure. Um…what else? You know this frustration grows over time. I got a restraining order against her for the three incidences. I mean, she used to call, sixty or seventy times a day. Sometimes a hundred times a day. It was absolutely ridiculous. I'm in grad school just trying to make it. It was just all bad.

One day she came by my house to drop off Tyler. I asked her to leave and she wouldn't leave. Out of frustration, I kind of picked her up and brought her out the front door and I said, "You got to leave." And then she was fighting to get back in the house, so I called the cops again. I said, "Look, I need some help. I need some relief." This was ridiculous. The straw that broke the camel's back was when I was talking to the person I was dating at the time, and she was all like, "Look, Drayke, the calls are never ending. You need to do something about it. Otherwise, I'm going to call her and talk to her."

My response was, "No, you don't need to." I was just so furious. I went over there, Mary, and I took her cell phone and I broke it. In that instance I was enraged. I broke her cell phone. She hit me, and I'm not proud of it, but we got into a shoving match. I left her apartment, called the police and I told them what happened. They met me at my house and they were like, "She's saying you punched her in the face and you kicked her." So she lied on the police report and I was arrested and I went to jail. Then subsequently, she used those same charges, went back to Texas, and sued me for sole custody. I lost custody of my child. I could only see him one week a year. I had a no-contact order form and I couldn't talk to him for six months. I had to go to anger management class for nine months. I mean, it's ridiculous. It's cost me like four thousand dollars in legal fees. I had two court cases; one going on in Texas and one in Atlanta. I was flying between both of them, trying to stay in school with limited resources. It was completely out of control.

My sister passed away five months after I went to jail and lost custody. Karla came down there for the funeral. I flew her and Tyler down because I thought it would be appropriate because they knew Gina (my sister). I thought it would be kind of a last good-bye. I guess Karla thought that was an opportunity to try and rekindle the relationship. So, I had to let her know, that's not how it's going down.

The most recent incident, up until that point, she had been unemployed for a year and a half. And with taxes due, I was like, "Well, look. I'll claim my son and give you $3,000 of the return. That way you have some cash to at least get on your feet." Well, I took some of the tax return money and flew out to see Tyler. I spent about $700 and I told her, "I'll give you $2,200 now and $800 later."

She said, "No, I'm mailing the check back. I called the IRS on you for fraud." She said that she did not agree to me signing the thing after she already agreed to it and now she's saying she didn't agree and that I should be expecting to hear from the IRS soon. According to her, I just committed fraud. I'm not the sole custodial parent. And this is after we discussed it. I was just trying to give her a hand because I knew she didn't have cash and this is how I'm treated.

"I can sense your frustration. Do you claim any ownership in what has transpired within this relationship?"
Mm-hmm.
Silence.
Yeah, it's funny because in my anger management class, it's been a great class, by the way. I recommend all men take that. You start unpacking your feelings. But anyhow, I felt a strong sense of pity for her, and that's something for me to figure out why. I just felt so bad. She lives in the projects of Atlanta. Like my son is there. All I wanted her to do was like get on her feet. I feel guilty for trying to succeed when I know my son is in the ghetto. So I guess I keep going back for seconds because I'm hoping that she can get on her feet

so he doesn't have to be in that environment anymore. I feel a little guilty, like maybe if I stayed with her, she wouldn't be in that position. I think because of some of the issues I have, I keep going back and just trying to help her out. But I failed to set proper boundaries and she deliberately set me up, in my opinion, just being very deliberate, setting up these conditions, which stated she could not be helped unless the help was coming from me. I knew that she needed help. I should have sought professional help for her as well as for myself.

"The question I'm prepared to ask requires in-depth self analysis. Reflect on your response before you provide an answer. Do you have the capacity to love another woman deeply?"

Okay, my capacity…I'll be honest. I feel much betrayed from my previous relationship. And secretly, if I come into a new encounter, I'm of the belief somebody has a motive. I used to take people as they were, but I honestly feel most women have a motive, like there is something they are trying to get out of the situation. And that's not fair. But my experience has taught me that I need to be very mindful, pay attention, like I'm looking for all of the red flags. I'm so focused on the negative that I don't think I give anybody a try. My first response when I feel uncomfortable is to just cut it off, to just cut the relationship off. I think I've developed that as a bad coping mechanism because I don't want to hurt anymore. And the easiest way not to hurt is at the first glance of that possibility, just to leave it alone. It hasn't been worth it. It's hard for me to take people at their word. I don't believe it. And I find myself asking for additional evidence from people like, "Tell me more about that." Like just double checking things I've heard just to be certain. I want to be sure that I'm getting what I think I'm getting. But that's not fair—making new people pay the price for something that happened to you in your past. I don't know. I'm very scared.

Silence.

I think my experience, (*pause*), absolutely tainted my perspective on love. I do want to love deeply. I do want to feel an emotion, a secure emotional connection, based on a mutual trust, a positive regard for another person. I don't trust that that's possible. For me, that makes me a cynical person in terms of the relationship front. And, you know, if it were up to me, I would have my son here. I'm just going to try and be the best dad I can be. I think I've resolved that if I'm not in a relationship, it's okay. I think that's where

I've gotten too. I've accepted that as a possible fate for me. Like I'm going to be solo and that's okay.

Silence.

Yeah, I think it's very difficult because of life's circumstance. I think my ability to connect closely with somebody has been jeopardized. Now, I mean, that doesn't mean that faith can't be restored and renewed, but…it's been damaged. It's in repair right now. It's in repair.

Silence.

"Does a man have the capacity to love more profoundly than a woman?"

Absolutely. I think men love more than women do. *Pause.* Not only do I feel like men love as deeply as women, but I feel like they love more. I feel like beneath all of this macho-ness that's within all of us, there is a soul that just wants to feel intimately connected with somebody else. I think we parade around here pretending, but it's just a big mask for a person who is emotionally starved of love. Honestly, I don't think our society or our women reward men for loving. We're rewarded for being strong, dominant, patriarchs. We're rewarded for being dominating. We're not rewarded for being affectionate. I've been affectionate with women and they think I'm gay. That's crazy. I think it challenges the stereotype. People are attracted to the stereotype of what a man should be rather than taking a man as what he is. It's a challenge for me.

Prolonged silence.

Mm-hmm. Mm-hmm. Yeah. I can just go on my friends, for example. I got a buddy of mine who is financially successful. I think women are attracted to him not because of who he is but because of the work he does, his ambitions and where he is going. The thing I always hear him say is, "You know women don't see me; they see the professional side that wants to do something. They see this other side. They don't take the time to see who I am." I sense a bitterness coming from him because he's frustrated because they're just intrigued by superficial characteristics across the board. You know, fame, money, etcetera. From my view, I would say I'm kind of the same. I share the same mindset. I don't know. It's just difficult to trust. I just feel like there's a capacity to be used. Sometimes I feel like women choose men just because there's a man shortage now. So it's like any guy will do, and that makes me feel very leery. And a lot of people are working with a stereotype of what a man should be and consequently, you'll get in a relationship where you'll get a lot of nagging. "You don't do this, you don't do that, you're not like this." If you take a person as they are, all that would be irrelevant.

I think we're scared not to be men, you know? Because from my experiences, if you turn down a girl, it's like, "Are you gay?" It's like, "No. I respect you enough that I don't want to participate in that kind of relationship with you." And that's a big driving fear. It's like how much emotion do you show? Where is the strength that some women may be attracted to? How do you preserve the strength, but also recognize that men are vulnerable too?

If we had men sit down and say how they felt every day, I don't think women would want to hear that. I don't know. We're rewarded for our aggression, our hard work and that's it honestly. Those are the things we're rewarded for. Being emotional and caring, I don't think we're rewarded for that. I don't think we have enough models to even teach us how to become that. I believe that we are all so very desperately wanting to be that on the inside. We're covering it up through drugs, alcohol or through working ourselves to death. You know what I mean? I think there's a voice there that has not developed. I think we have emotions that we cannot communicate because we do not have the words to express them and the only acceptable outlet seems to be in the form of anger. That's my opinion. I don't know. I don't know.

Silence.

I have more to say, but that was a tough question, Mary. There was a movie that came out with T.D. Jakes called "Not Easily Broken." It was… insightful as it pertains to men's capacity to love women. I would say that the capacity is very strong, very real, but it's hidden because we are scared. We are scared to love. There is nothing we desire more. I would also argue that women are also starving for love, but they don't know how to love either and I think those two inabilities together are preventing us from getting more of what it is we both deserve.

"Thank you for your honesty."

It was my pleasure.

COLOR ~~BLIND~~

I prayed to God to give me a sign and HE DID. This wonderful woman made my vision transparent and amplified all the florescent colors of the rainbow when she stepped into my life. You know the saying "You do not know someone unless you have seen their true colors". THANK GOD I'm no longer color blind or else these tainted shades of BLUE, GREEN AND RED would have permeated my positive aura. Being oblivious to the signs would have left me spiritually depleted, mentally cheated and emotionally unfulfilled..... Ladies/Gentlemen please DO NOT become naive when the colors are right in front of your face.

— CheyNaRey

Zayven

CHAPTER FIVE
The Rebound Guy

Zodiac Sign: Libra
Approximate Age: Thirties
Occupation: Ph.D. Candidate
Passions: Love, Family, the Bible, Education,
Finance and Music
Hobbies: Learning, Reading, Singing, Watching
Sports and Socializing

"I knew that I was the rebound because I was giving a lot of myself and doing a lot of things that most men don't really do and it would not be reciprocated. You know when someone really wants you and wants you for who you are. So, a lot of the time it was me giving, giving and reaching out, or really being there and the person was more nonchalant. That helped to validate that I was the rebound. Like I said, when a woman loves a man, she will give. You know?

She will be reciprocating. That's what I've been learning because of my mother and my father's relationship. I know my mother loves my father because of what she's taken, has been through and been there for him and you can see that because of how she cares for him. But with this person, it wasn't that. It was, "This guy's a nice guy, so I'm going to like him. I mean, he's nice, but it's not like this is the guy that I really care about and I want to be with. I love this man no matter what." It wasn't like that." —Zayven

"How were you raised to treat a woman?"

I don't think it was a formal thing where I was told, "Okay, this is how you treat a woman." But I learned through observing my community and my father and my mother. And basically it was more of, "You take care of the wife, you take care of the woman, you always provide for her." That's basically what I mainly saw. I didn't see much of the emotional part of it because my parents didn't really display it. I didn't see them actually do that kind of stuff. It was more they had roles. My mother was the nurturer, the home person who took care of the home, and my father was like the breadwinner who was outside working. Their relationship was based on an understanding. Each understood what they were both supposed to do and I understood. I saw my father taking care of my mother in that sense. But I didn't really see a lot of the emotional stuff. You know, the way to take care of someone emotionally. But I saw that you should provide for the woman and provide for the family. So that's what I observed. What I learned otherwise, was from outside—watching television, seeing other couples, and hearing about other couples, and reading and observing outside that women are built differently from men and they have more needs than men. So that kind of constitutes how I was raised to treat a woman. You can sum it up as my primary socialization and my secondary socialization.

"Describe your first experience with love?"

My first experience with love would probably come about when I was I think thirteen.

It was a different feeling because it was something where I actually really wanted to see this person every moment and I felt very happy just being with her. I'd never felt that way before. So, it was mostly the joy of knowing that the person is there, seeing the person and always wanting to be around the person, and you get kind of like drawn to that person. So that's what I knew and that's what I felt. It was something that I never experienced before and I would do a lot of stuff; I'd write poetry. I'd write letters. I would want to bring flowers and I've seen this in movies, so it made me want to get her attention and I would do these things. I just wanted to be around her. I wanted to be close to her. I think that was pretty much it. It was very interesting.

When I moved into my high school years, I was thinking as a mature teenager. I wasn't thinking of marriage and all that fancy stuff. It was more of trying to fit in with everyone. From my observation, everyone had relationships. Everybody had a girlfriend or boyfriend, so it seemed like the norm and I guess it was just like the norm. But I did have relationships. I dated; however, I didn't put a lot of myself into it because I was learning about women at that time too. I wasn't taught by my father. He never sat down and had "the discussion" or anything. I was kind of learning through experiences. So, it was mostly dating, learning different things about women, what they want and what they like and how to approach women. I was never the kind of person who would have any kind of disrespectful approach to a woman. I was always able to have good conversations with women. I was always able to compliment women and allow them to feel good about themselves. I never had in any way, shape or form any kind of relationship where I turned my back on someone or treated someone like they were dirt. I didn't do that. We mutually dated new people, moved on, or it was just like nothing to the extreme where I was some kind of guy who never cared. I always had a caring side to me. I always cared about people's feelings. I always cared about any girl that I dated. I did not date anyone I didn't care about. Um, and that was in high school. Coming up in college, it was the same thing. I dated people I cared about and I've learned that when a woman loves you and she wants you, she will do whatever for you, because people go after who they love and women go after whom they love. That's why sometimes they will end up dating a bad guy and you won't understand, but it's because they love that person, that's why. They gravitate toward that person.

My college experience was basically just the same experience—dating, trying to understand more, maturing, having a different perspective on how relationships work and having a more seriousness toward relationships, not just dating with a sense of being in the norm, like everyone being popular, having girlfriends or dating or whatever. It was trying to find some stability, something that then you can look toward, probably marriage because that's when I started formulating my own perception—perceptions of how someday I just might want to settle down and perhaps find my wife in college. That was in undergrad. But again, I wasn't sure and again my male hormones were on high alert. I wasn't sure if I wanted that so I was still searching and dating and didn't really get into anything serious.

My relationships were different when I got to graduate school because I actually was in Jamaica and I got to the University of Virginia in 2004. So all of my undergrad relationships and high school relationships were back home in Jamaica. My first relationship when I got here was with a Christian young lady. She was really focused on her relationship with God and I knew I was interested the first time I saw her and saw her eyes. She had really bright, beautiful eyes. I wanted to know her. A friend of mine knew her and she had this bubbly, high spirit and I was like wow. So a friend of mine introduced us and I pursued her. It was mutual and we dated for a while. But back home in Jamaica I'd had a bad relationship that I had just gotten out of because the person I was with cheated on me. So, it was really hard for me to even consider if I was ready to commit again because I had thought that my heart could be broken again. When I left Jamaica, in some ways I was kind of scared to commit due to my past relationship.

"Please provide a visual picture of that relationship."
That relationship was the last I experienced before I came to Virginia. It was very hurtful. I have never cried over

someone or something that much. I remember crying, but I have never actually felt so hurt and really disappointed. I mean, there were times when I would stay in my room and not come out. I would write in journals or I would cry in my room because I felt like I'd allowed myself to fall for this person, but at the same time I found out that the person was like me when I was younger. They were like me when I wasn't ready to commit. You know, I was just doing me and wasn't ready to commit, just dating and stuff. But I guess it came back to me that women too are becoming more like men.

"How so?"

They too are searching, and they too are not really committed. But that kind of hurt me because this is when I was kind of having my transformation. I was thinking about being with one person and that kind of changed the perception I had established for myself because of my past hurt and not knowing if that could happen again, or if I would be able to open up like that again without thinking that someone would probably hurt me again like that. I was at a low. I had a lot of low moments. There were times when I just remembered having flashbacks and just saying wow. Visualizing what she would do with the other person, like that movie "The Best Man," when the guy was seeing his wife with his best friend and crying. It was almost like that. I could see pictures, graphic pictures, and I would just cringe, you know? So, it was hard for me and I had to leave. I felt like if I didn't leave the country and come away that it would have been hard for me to even get over that situation. So, that's what that did to me. It kind of scared me in a way, where I didn't know if I believed in this whole committed love thing.

So, now to continue with the relationships I had in grad school. I met this young lady who I thought was really attractive, because sometimes that's the first thing you see. You see the physical, something that you like about the person, whether it's their personality that's vibrant or whether it's their appearance. I asked a friend about her and the friend actually introduced us. But in some way, after dating I was still learning more about myself and if I was ready. I was reminiscing on what I had been through and what I believed and what I had felt. In some ways I wasn't ready to be vulnerable, to really fall in love because of my experiences. I just wasn't sure. So, we dated for a little bit and it didn't really go far. That was the first relationship, my first encounter. After that, I kind of actually was upset with myself because then I had someone who was a good person for me. I even found myself thinking about marriage or trying harder, or you know, just allowing myself to fall in love again, which I didn't. So after that I started saying, "You know what? I can't let this thing keep me down about not being willing to fall in love because of what happened to me back home." So, I met another young lady who I dated, who I actually allowed myself to fall for, and I really went out of my way.

I think my love language is kind of more like giving deeds and trying to show my care and compassion. So, I did all of those things, and that's how I show a lot of my love, by doing things. I help. I am there when you need me. I'll drop anything that I'm doing to be there for you and that's when I knew that I was actually falling in love with this girl. So we dated, but again, that girl that I dated actually just got out of a relationship with a guy she deeply loved. Me being the person that that I am, I did all that I could to show her the depth of my love, but I knew I was the "rebound" guy.

"How did your actions help to support your conclusion of being the rebound guy?"

I knew that I was the rebound because I was giving a

lot of myself and doing a lot of things that most men don't really do and it would not be reciprocated. You know when someone really wants you and wants you for who you are. So, a lot of the time it was me giving, giving and reaching out, or really being there and the person was more nonchalant. That helped to validate that I was the rebound. Like I said, when a woman loves a man, she will give. You know? She will be reciprocating. That's what I've been learning because of my mother and my father's relationship. I know my mother loves my father because of what she's taken, has been through and been there for him and you can see that because of how she cares for him. But with this person, it wasn't that. It was, *"This guy's a nice guy, so I'm going to like him. I mean, he's nice, but it's not like this is the guy that I really care about and I want to be with. I love this man no matter what."* It wasn't like that.

After she graduated, well, we broke up before she graduated, and then she went back home. So, after that I met another young lady who was in grad school. Both ladies that I met before, they were both in undergrad. So I met this young lady who came to the University of Virginia for grad school and I actually had one or two more semesters left. I was finished with my coursework, so I had a little bit of time to play with, in a way. So, I met some students who were in my degree. They were first-year computer science students in the master's program and one of them was actually staying on campus and she had roommates, like three roommates. So, as a part of this introducing myself and knowing the new students and having them know me, a couple of us went out and the young lady who was in my course told us to come back to her dorm, so we went. Then I saw this young lady in one of the rooms, and physically she caught my eye. I wanted to be introduced to her, which I was. And ever since that day, we never left each other's company. I even dropped all my friends, my guy friends that I had. They didn't see me. If it was lunch, if it was the movies, if it was the mall, I was calling her, finding out what she was doing or she was calling me finding out what I was doing and then we would hang out. But what I learned during that time was that she was in a relationship, a long distance relationship. So when she told me that she was in a relationship and some of the things she had to deal with, I knew that she never felt wanted or appreciated. I felt like I could have done better. Plus I was giving of myself because I really liked this person, and I wanted to do better. I wanted to do more than what that person was doing. And I was right there on campus, and he wasn't. He was somewhere in some other state. So, I think what happened is that, again,

I'm a person who gives and I show my heart to someone based on how I am. I care. I'm there for you if you need me. I'll be there and you can call on me. After a couple of months, we were still kind of dating on the side. She didn't break off the relationship yet and her boyfriend would come to campus and I couldn't show myself because, of course, he didn't know anything about me.

"How did you cope with this situation?"

I felt a little bit cheated because I was settling for something that I didn't have to, but I wanted what I wanted and I felt like this was the person I wanted to get to know and I was falling for. In some way I was hoping that her relationship with him would have ended and we would have gotten together.

So, like I was saying about the other person who she was still with, I think for men it's really hard to accept that the person who they love, or the women that they want to be with has somebody else. I think men are like lions in some ways. They like to have their own territory and not have anyone else in that territory. They want to be the only one who is in that territory or in command. They don't like to share a person, especially a woman. So, I think it was hard because it actually damaged my ego and hurt my feelings in a way because I saw something that I wanted, but the person seemed like she wanted that guy. But because he wasn't putting out enough effort, then I was the next best thing.

"The next best thing, while strong words, are they appropriate?"

Yes, I felt like the "next best thing," but not the thing that she wanted. I felt like number two, in a way, and no man likes to feel like number two. You always want to be King George, first king, only king, no other king. I felt like I had to play that role and stay on the back burner, in the shadows until whatever was sorted out. At the same time, I was still making myself fall [for her] and making myself into this person, not knowing if it was going to work or not. I kept showing my interest and that I was there for her. I really cared about her and I spent a lot of time with her and this was what she couldn't have gotten from the primary person. I too brought it up to her. I said, "What are you waiting for? I'm here. Obviously I want to be with you."

After a while I think she decided to move on. I think it was a couple of months after we were seeing each other when they broke up. I had thought that she told him about me, but it was obvious that she didn't tell him about me, or that she was seeing someone else.

I remember one time he came to campus and we were in church and she saw him sitting across the hall and she got up from beside me and went outside. That behavior was kind of odd to me because if you've moved on and you're with someone new, it doesn't matter if that person you were with comes or whatever. So, eventually I kept giving of myself. I fell in love. I finished college and came up to New York and was working while she was still working on her master's. We had our little challenges, but we would see each other. I would come to the university and she would come to New York. It was 2006 when officially we started dating; we started having the title of boyfriend-girlfriend. It was 2006 of October when I actually proposed. We met in 2005. I knew before I proposed that this person was the person I wanted to be married to. I spent two Christmases with her family before that. The first Christmas she was still with her boyfriend. The second Christmas she wasn't. When she brought me home for Christmas I got to see their family structure. They were a church family. They were really, really a church family. They seemed really nice, and I like the fact that she had a good upbringing. I saw that as something that my kids could learn from her, because she had this kind of Christian background and this church upbringing. She was good with kids. I saw her with her niece and nephews.

Just looking at her, every time I see her, it puts a smile on my face. When you love someone, you wake up seeing them asleep and you will start smiling to yourself because it's a beautiful sight to see that person. That's how I felt. I just know that I was into this person so I prayed. I fasted for two days. Before we even got married, before I had proposed to her, we had broken up for like a week or two, but I had already planned and had already prayed and was getting the ring and everything. When I spoke to her the time after that, I was trying to get back and mend things, but I had already had the ring and I was driving from New York. I drove all the way from New York to the university and proposed to her, so that was kind of reuniting the relationship after two weeks or so. My mind never changed. My heart never changed. I knew I wanted to be with this person no matter what. No matter what happened, whatever argument happened, whatever way I felt, my feelings were always renewed. Every day is just a new sheet. You're starting over. Your love is renewed and your care is renewed. It's not like I bring anything over [from the day before.] The day has passed and my love is refreshed and new, renewed again.

I realize that women are not like that. They will remember and keep things with them. I was watching a sermon this morning and the pastor said, "Men can compartmentalize. They can lock things away. They can put things away. But women, they will remember things." So even if tomorrow you're thinking that two days ago something happened and it's already on the back burner, she will still be reminded of it. She reminds herself of it.

So, even though we had broken up, I proposed and she said yes. And again I still felt like I was really putting myself out there. It was about how I felt about this person, but there were some doubts that I had because when I met her, her heart belonged to another. She always talked about how much she admired her ex-boyfriend. She didn't have that much admiration for me. Their relationship was more of a cordial relationship, where I could see that she really looked up to this guy. She spoke about him and how he was, and sometimes I'd try to compare myself and I felt like I wasn't treated the same way or looked upon the same way. So that reality remained in the back of my mind. I knew that things weren't perfect, but I loved her and there wasn't anyone else I wanted to be with. She was "that" person, so I went ahead and married her in 2007, August 18th.

"Are your issues pertaining to being second place, her plan B, resolved?"

Basically, the issues about me feeling second place, I thought would have passed, but it kept on. It kept on revisiting, coming back in my memory because the ex-boyfriend wasn't fully out the picture. He was still present. They were still calling each other and texting each other while we were engaged. He told her that he still loved her and she told me that and it was hard for me to deal with because I felt like she had dealt with that and that it was over with. So in a way, I kind of felt insecure. I felt like, "This is the person that I'm compared to because he was the last person you were with and obviously it feels kind of awkward to know that he still feels that way about you and you are still having a kind of relationship or communication and it makes me feel like I'm not being treated the way you told me you treated him in your relationship."

I think I felt like the love that I had for her was pure. But, for me to marry someone who I had doubts about was an issue. I wondered if she could love me in the way I deserved. It's just the fact that my love was so strong and I was focused on wanting to really make this person happy, wanting to love this woman, wanting to take care of her. I should have been focused on whether she was loving me the way I deserve. There was doubt, but I didn't focus on that. What I did was look at the attributes that I really valued in her, and the way I felt and I made my decision based on that. So, my decision was based upon the emotions that I felt about her, and just some things that I really valued as important, my criteria of the qualities a good wife should have and she possessed those. So, that's why I went ahead with the marriage because of those reasons.

We never went on a honeymoon. We both actually fell asleep at her father's house [after the wedding]. We didn't even sleep in the same room because we actually were working, cleaning up the church after the wedding. We got married, we moved into a place in New Jersey, and we had our disagreements. I had my way of doing things and she had her way of how she thought things should be done, so we had a lot of combativeness back and forth. Like she didn't agree with how I would say things to her, so I would try to learn and work on how I would express myself because I was just now learning that words were so important to her. She was very sensitive, so even if I said something jokingly or something slightly sounding like anyway to her, she would probably check me or I would get an attitude or something. So I was starting to learn that our communication was really kind of off in some ways.

I think before we got married, she told me that she married with the intention of me changing some things or she didn't like some things but was hoping they would change. I think if you marry someone, you have to be in love with this person not even thinking about changing them or whatever, because if you think like that, there's going to be issues because you're not going to be fully pleased until those changes happen. I feel like things happen over time.

So in the marriage it was okay. We had two different perspectives. Our cultures were different. She felt like I probably treated her like I was her father because of certain issues. I had the butterfly feeling and knowing that you love each other and then you start looking at the rational part, you know, the money management, building, buying a house, paying bills, and I didn't learn these things. I didn't even do a credit check on my wife. I didn't know her credit score. I didn't know these things. I'm coming from Jamaica. I married for love and that's it. But you know those things were issues. Money was an issue, managing, you know, she and myself too. I had an issue with some ways that she would talk to me. I wasn't a person who would verbally curse or whatever. I didn't do that. What I learned is that like my father and my mother, they had the same type of dynamics. My father is rough and he would say whatever and was really kind of coarse and her mother was similar. It wasn't her father but her mother who would say whatever, whether it hurt your feelings or not. I felt like she would be like that with me. She would be really strict and we would just say things to each other that would just hurt each other. That was something that I felt was an issue because we were both independent, educated people who felt like no one could've backed down, no one backed off. We both had a point to prove or we both had something to say.

So this is just by living with each other, consistently going back and forth and my relationship and my intimacy was seldom. It wasn't much like two persons wanting to take part; it was like me wanting something and you were like, "Okay, let me do my duty as a wife" and that's it. It wasn't, "Okay, I'm so into you that I want to be intimate with you or be with you." I could feel her lack of passion for me. She wouldn't even kiss me during our most intimate moments.

"How did that restriction on intimacy impact you?"

I felt like she didn't kiss me because she didn't have the passion for me. Like I said, when someone is in love, they'll give their all. When a woman loves, she'll do whatever she needs to do and she will give her all and she will put herself into it. I didn't feel like she had the passion or compassion. I don't know if that's how she loved, but this is a lot of the minor things that happened where even my touching and stuff was a tickle. Everything was a tickle for her, so I couldn't touch her like that. I couldn't be very caressing. I'm very affectionate and I like to be caressed and for her that was an issue. Kissing, I would have to ask her to kiss me. I would have to ask to do certain things and it was so mechanical, you know? So, I felt that we started really deteriorating even before we got married because I felt like I was chasing something. I was more chasing than allowing something to be mutual, or knowing if something is really mutual.

"And this left you feeling…"

It made me feel neglected. It made me feel less of a husband, and I didn't know how to deal with that. So, the dynamics changed between me and my wife. She said I didn't know how to love her in the way she wanted to be loved. I didn't know her love language and I wasn't getting it, so each time I would try to learn and get it, it's like, "You're not getting it," so I felt put down a lot of times, and at the same time I started feeling like I was putting her down too because she wasn't getting it for me either. So we both weren't getting what we needed from each other and I felt neglected.

Even though I was put down and stuff, I still loved her. I still loved her and I was still determined to learn her love language. I would beg her. I would say, "Tell me. Teach me. I want to get this." She would reply, "You won't get it. You're not going to get it." It was really frustrating. I would just be at work sometimes trying to figure out how to get it, and I couldn't focus on my work. I would just want to get it more than working. That's what I'd think about. I'd be at work and just want to get home to practice to see if I could get it. You know what I mean? So, most of my days were like, "I can't wait to get home because I really want to work on this relationship. I want to be around my wife. I want to really try." But each time it was like I was failing to reach her expectations. It really kind of felt disappointing and kind of at the same time I felt neglected because I knew how things could have been, and it wasn't. I was neglected and I felt that I wasn't loved. I even told her a couple of times, "I don't think you love me. I don't think you love me the way you loved your ex-boyfriend." I brought that up because of something that happened in the relationship, where I had seen text messages in her phone and I asked her who it was and she told me it was a friend she knew from the Navy, and she told me the person's name. But I knew the ex-boyfriend's name, so she didn't tell me that name. The number was stored in the phone as an initial, like a code name. She called me at work the very same evening and told me that she lied to me; it was actually her ex- boyfriend. That really upset me and validated what I was feeling before: she wasn't over him. I don't know why this person kept coming back into our relationship and I kind of felt like it was taboo [karma], you know, because she probably did him wrong and it's coming back to haunt us. I didn't know what it was. She told me that she was upset that she didn't get over the fact that she felt like she cheated on him. I didn't understand that either because you moved on with your life. You got married. So why is it that an issue? The only way it would matter is if you care about this person still. So, that was something that kind of led me to feel even more like a second place or not a priority, or not really at the forefront or not really someone who, "Okay, I have passion for you and you're the person I want to be with." You know, it just went bad from there.

What I am going through now is accepting that the relationship is going to be over. We separated December [of 2008]. We didn't separate based on I was abusing her or doing anything abusive; it was just that she felt that she was unhappy.

Something that I neglected to mention was that my wife is an identical twin. Prior to my marriage I didn't understand the dynamics of twins. Now I have more insight. I don't know if it's different for every twin, but her twin sister has always been a part of our relationship, so it was not only unclear if she loved me as she loved her ex-boyfriend or if she still loves him but also competing with her twin sister was exhausting because her twin sister also lived in New York. I know the Bible talks about "leave and cleave" to your husband and stuff, but their bond was so strange that it came above our marriage. She denied it and she said, "It's two different relationships. It's not really greater than or less." How I felt was her twin sister was always just there. I felt like we never resolved anything whenever we had a disagreement or an argument. She would leave the house, pack her stuff, and go over to New York to her twin sister's and then I'd end up driving all the way to New York at 12 or 1 in the morning, going back to her, asking her to come home. That happened more than twice, more than three times. The fact that she was consistently leaving and going there, she had a crutch. She never stayed when the heat was in the kitchen, never committed to working things out.

Her twin sister enabled her. It was not a situation where I physically touched her, so I feel like if two people are married, you should allow them to work their stuff out. Not saying that she should be a bad sister, because they're twin sisters and I had to understand that they have a special bond, which I was learning. But because I was unsure of my position or where I was in the priority list, it kind of mattered to me. So we separated and she moved to her twin sister's and it's been almost ten months now.

"Did you two employ any marital interventions?"

I think interventions were needed after we separated. We tried to go to counseling in New York, doing like five or six sessions. While in sessions she was saying she was one foot outside the door and she had told me before that her ex-boyfriend treated her better than me. During each therapy session it was the same thing, no kind of breakthrough or kind of wanting to work things out. I was really trying to ask her to come back home. I'd say, "Let's go to counseling. Let's work things out," and she was consistently saying, "No, no, no."

During that time, I lived in New Jersey and she was in New York and I was looking to move to New York. So at the end of the lease in New Jersey, we both cleaned the apartment and we were looking to move. I was thinking when we moved to our new place, we were going to move in together and then we were going to start doing counseling and then going to start working on things, but then she told me she wasn't going to sign the lease and she didn't think she needed to invest in the relationship because it wasn't going anywhere.

"How did her words impact you?"

You know, it kind of really shook me in a really bad way. I felt really down. I went through some periods where I was semi-depressed. I didn't feel motivated to do a lot of things. Eventually, I had to tell my sister that this was going on. I had to reach out and get help from my youngest sister. I'm in school full-time; my income was not enough for me to get a place for myself, so I needed help... my wife's help. But my sister allowed me to come stay with her, and that's where I am right now. That kind of felt like my wife was turning her back on me and on the marriage. I struggled with that for a little bit because I still wanted to work things out, and was hoping that things were working out. But in March or so I found myself calling her and she wouldn't call me. I was in the hospital and she didn't know that. She didn't communicate with me. I was always calling her and a friend of mine, my best friend at my wedding, he was like, "That's not right because you and her didn't have a bitter breakup."

I could see if we'd had a bitter breakup and this person is horrible and you don't want to talk to him, but we didn't have that kind of parting, so why is it that she can't even show that she cares?

"Describe your internal struggle."

I struggled with that because I felt like it was kind of strange that we couldn't even have a conversation like, "Hey, how are you?" I mean, I know things were going on. It was like distancing herself. I was calling and when I called her voice sounded like, "I don't really want to talk to you. I don't really have much to say to you," like resentment. I felt like I was blaming myself the whole time, so I was down a lot of times because I felt like it was my fault. Then when I started to feel like that, I started reminiscing back on some of the things that I've done, some mistakes that I've made. I could have made better choices in my life. I started feeling like I should not be blaming myself because it takes two to tango. It takes two persons to make anything work. I feel that you fall in love by chance, you stay in love by work, and you fall out of love by choice.

"When it's all said and done, do you hold any responsibility?"

The responsibility that I hold is that I should have been more patient with deciding or going ahead with getting into marriage. I think I should have been patient in terms of… not even patient but be more vigilant and more aware, looking at the positive and weighing everything and doing a proper analysis. Because you can analyze everything in a short time and you can take a long time to analyze too. But you must analyze; that's the thing. I think I didn't do a good comprehensive analysis of weighing how I felt. Also, our communication, doing more checks to see if I could live with these things or if this person really wanted to spend the rest of their lives or the rest of their time with me or, you know, how she felt about certain things. I didn't spend a lot of time doing that and I think that it was my responsibility because I was the one who actually called her father, called my mother, and got both of their approval three weeks before I proposed. I had time to really think about it and seeing that we were broken up and stuff and I still went ahead, got the ring, and still went and proposed. I should have taken that time to really, really let things just kind of settle with me and really assess things. So, I think that was my responsibility. I should have taken the issues between us more seriously back then because I really value marriage. I am a Christian and I struggle with the fact that I didn't get married to get a divorce.

One of the sermons that I watched when I was doing my divorce is that sometimes we don't know what we want and we go off our feelings, but we have to do the assessment to see if this person is our equal part, to see if we are evenly yoked or not. And I think it takes time to spend with yourself and it takes time to spend assessing that relationship with that person. I think now I am seeing and learning that you have to make sure that both of you are in love with each other. It's not easy, but it has to be something you are sure about like, "This person really loves me and I love her." Then you can take it from there, trying to assess the other things. I was sure that I was in love with my wife. I think I was too much in love with her, and I think that kind of made me overlook what I should have been getting. I think that this time it's my responsibility to not overlook it and make sure I'm getting what I need.

Well, I mean, other stuff I could share is that it wasn't very fulfilling. It wasn't very fulfilling for me. I enjoyed intimacy, I enjoyed sex, and I enjoyed being around her. I enjoyed trying to do nice things for her. When I go to the mall, if I shop for myself or if I don't shop for myself, I take back something for her. While at work, I would probably send a card or write a poem. At home I would cook dinner, have candles lit all over the house and stuff. I wanted to take trips with her. I wanted to do stuff, but it felt like I was giving, giving, giving, giving, but I wasn't getting. It's like when you go to China and you speak English. No matter how you speak English, whatever way you speak English, they're not going to understand if they don't speak English. So, whatever I was doing wasn't any big deal. I was trying to do that and at the same time trying to learn. I think it shouldn't be that hard, so it wasn't really fulfilling for me and I don't think it was very fulfilling for her either. In a lot of ways it was draining, because I wanted to be pleased and I wanted to be taken care of, which she did in some ways, and she tried in some ways, but it was more like a chore. But I really, really wanted to make her happy and do stuff for her. It wasn't a chore for me; it was something that I felt in me to do. So that's it. That's how I know I'm in love, when I'm compelled to do something for someone even when they did me wrong. They could call me and say, "Can you do this for me?" and I would still do it or I would think about doing something, instead of being mean, and I would try to accommodate.

Even this one time when me and my wife were separated, I found out that she was talking to someone very late in the morning, early in the morning… some guy. I don't think it was the ex-boyfriend, but it was someone else. And even then, I still didn't cut her off. I still was kind. I didn't do things that would be vindictive. I actually told her, "Since you are talking to someone else, you should get your own plan. I feel it's kind of disrespectful if you want to do that. I mean, this is our family and you are entertaining someone else and I don't feel comfortable with that plan." So I told her, "You can get your own phone. I'm not going to disconnect the phone until you get your own phone." I think in that case I was accommodating. Most people I told were telling me to cut the line off and don't ask any questions, but I didn't do that.

"My question to you is, why accommodate this behavior?"

I think I was trying to line up my actions with what Christ would want me to do. I think I was trying to show compassion even though I was hurt. You know, I know I've done wrong. God has forgiven me in many ways. I mean, I'm no way near perfect, you know? I felt like even though

I got upset and I would say things and she would say things, as I said, my love was renewed. The next day, I could still forgive and still want to show you that same care. I would still want to work on things. I would still want to love you even more. So, I think doing that was me trying to not be vindictive, kind of a mixture of accommodating her and not trying to be mean because I knew that she needed a phone and why would I cut the phone off? That's not right. Even though she's doing what she's doing, she needs a phone too. So, I just told her, "Once you get the new phone, just call me and then I'll disconnect it [the old one]." That, to me, is being civil. I think in a way that I'm diplomatic. I want to keep the peace. I want to work out things where it's civil. Being nasty didn't make any sense.

"These compromises, were you looking for a positive resolution?"

Um…that's a good question because that was my hope. I've always placed my heart on the line, disregarding and trying to compromise and trying to not really look at what I want or what I should get because I don't think I'm a selfish person. I should have done better in looking at what I needed and what I should get. I started looking at things and I said, "I do hope my marriage works. But is that what I want? Do I really want to be with this person?" It's one thing to want to save my marriage and it's another thing to envision myself spending the rest of my life with this person. Did I feel that this was a person that I could spend the rest of my life with? I looked at all the things and I looked at what's been said and what we've been going through and I really believe that it was best that we went our separate ways.

I never thought I would have gotten to this point, but looking at all the data and looking at all the things that happened, if it's not two persons trying to have the passion to save their marriage and they love each other, it's going to be very hard. If my wife could be away for nine months, or we could be away from each other for nine months, it's not a good thing.

Friday was the first I saw my wife in almost five months. I mean, she wasn't even calling me. I called her on her birthday. I called her once or twice, but it was just like that. You would think that we were probably archrivals or enemies, which is not how it was because I stayed away. Why? Because I wanted her to have time to think about what she really wanted. Because whenever I used to go around her, initially I would ask her to come back to our home. I would get frustrated and I would say, "This is not right, you know?" Then we would get into an argument and she'd tell me to leave and don't come back, don't talk to her. So I would go because I didn't want her to get upset. I would end up going on the train, crying to myself, or crying and leaving because I felt really hurt that we were going through this. I've never felt like that before. I've never got into an argument and then felt like I am breaking down. *Why are we arguing like this? Why is it so hard?* You know? And I think it made me feel so drained. So I feel like after looking at everything, I was the one that needed to accept that it's over because she had already accepted that. So, I had to get to this point and it took me a long while, but I think that I'm at the point where I'm being rational. God didn't put us together for us to be apart, but it happens. And I have to know that life is not perfect and when life throws lemons at you, you make lemonade. That's how it goes. But when things happen, you try to make the best of it and try to learn from it.

Whether we get back together, and I'm not saying we can't, but if it happens, it'd have to be a concerted effort where both persons really come together and really try to work out things or decide that they're going to work on themselves and try to make things work. But if that's not going to happen, then it's not going to work.

"Did this production dismantle your belief system as it pertains to love?"

I do believe in love after all this. I always believed in love. I have friends who call me Cupid because they know I am actually big on love and relationships. In high school and undergrad years, I was a musician and a lot of the things I used to want to sing about or write about were relationships and love. I felt like it was a beautiful thing for two persons to have this same feeling for each other and love each other and want to be with each other forever. You know, that's wonderful. It's just that if you find that right person who's not perfect but is perfect for you, great. So I do believe in love. I just feel like I haven't found that person. I know I can find that person, though. Some people get it the first time;

some people get it the second time. I do have the capacity to love again. I'm just more awakened that it could happen to me. It happened to me. Just like this happened to me like I wasn't above anything. It doesn't have to mean that it's the end of the world, but it did happen. It either can make you or break you, and I'm not going to let it break me because I feel that one of the biggest things in me is me wanting to be an advocate for good relationships and love. That's why I don't think it's going to be impossible or hard for me to find love. I will not stop believing in love, not at all.

"What is your opinion about why some women hold the belief that some men don't have the capacity to love deeply?"

I think the reason why some women don't believe that men can love as deeply as they do is because men have a different kind of perspective on love. I think women are more emotional and men can be emotional too, but they are givers and women are receivers. So women define love based on how they receive. Men define love based on how they give, and if it's received. Also men like to receive too, but their nature is givers. The two don't really cross all the time because women expect to get love based on "Okay, are my emotional needs being met?" A lot of stuff is based on getting things, getting things, getting things. I think the perception is both male and female should stop and learn the nature of each other. Women should learn how to give while receiving, and men should learn how to receive and give, because that's how you would understand both sides. A lot of times men give, give, give, give and they don't receive. I always use this analogy: a lot of men go to go-go bars or gentlemen's clubs because they receive. They receive attention and they receive this kind of feeling where they feel like the woman is all about them and not about anybody else. I believe that a lot of women don't treat their men like that, so they put a lot of pressure on the man to keep giving and learning and giving, but a lot of women don't try to give their men, or try and please their man in a way that he could understand how to receive, so he could know how to give her what she needs to receive.

Men can love deeply and when a man loves deeply, he will do anything. He would even try going to the mindset of a woman to try and learn her, and that's the man who would take up a book to research and read and try and find out more about women and the man who would not be afraid to cry or express himself, or try to get emotional with his wife or the person he's with.

Mary, a lot of men feel like they have to be macho and be hard because they think that's the persona we need to show. If we cry, we're weak. If we want to cuddle or hug, we're weak. If we watch a girly movie with our wives, we're girly, we're weak. If we write poetry, we're weak. If we wash our hair, we're feminine. If we comb our hair, we're feminine. If we want to wash our underwear or whatever... I don't care about any of those things. I can do all of those things. So, I think that once we understand the nature of both sexes and men are not so caught up in machismo and giving more internally, a better understanding can evolve. Most important, men need to connect with their emotional side. And I believe that women can actually get in touch with the side where they don't always want to receive and focus on giving. When this occurs, I think there will be a balance.

To expand on my previous thoughts, I do believe that a man can love deeply as a woman. If a man is emotionally strong and just as committed to letting go and really giving into the love that he feels, it's more powerful than what a woman feels, more powerful than you could ever imagine. I would like to see the statistics of men who have hurt themselves over love. I'm not saying that's a healthy mindset, but they must have really loved that person. That's why men do these things. I think when a man is in love, his love is deeper. A woman can move on more easily than a man, because women can express themselves emotionally.

They know how to do that. They know how to vent; men don't. So when men love deeply, they don't know how to express it emotionally as well as a woman. But I think men do love very deeply though. Reflecting back, I saw this movie, "The Notebook." Even though it's a movie, it shows that a man can have a love, a great, great love, for a woman that is so deep that he would spend the rest of his life inside a nursing home with his wife, and live there. I mean, men have the capacity to love like that. A man would give his life for his wife...

"What is your perspective on soul mates?"

If a man can keep someone as a soul mate and still fall in love with someone else while knowing that someone else is his soul mate, that's deep. I'm thinking that if my ex was my soul mate, I couldn't have been able to move on, but I'm moving on. I felt like I really was in love with this person, and I felt like my love was sincere. After assessing everything and rationalizing everything, I'm now concluding that my soul mate is actually out there. So I don't think a man, knowing that his soul mate is out there and she is available, would not want to be without her. I think that he would really want to go after her. He would still want to be with her. If he should get with somebody else, it's probably his greatest hope that this person would help him to move on or hoping that this is temporary or just killing time until things work out with the soul mate. If the soul mate is still there, eventually he's going to have to decide to either deal with her or emotionally move on. I don't think of a soul mate as a particular person but a particular kind of character or criteria. I would say a wife like the Proverbs 31 woman is the soul mate for me. Because that's how you have to look at how the Bible describes a mate and how you describe that woman to be the kind of woman you want to be with. I don't really understand the whole concept of this soul mate thing. I believe that you can find someone who fits what you want for a wife or a person to be with and then you and that person can have a bond or a love that surpasses anything. The term soul mate is kind of making it too mechanical, or "I have to find this one person." I don't think it's one person. I think it's a kind of person. It's an umbrella that someone fits under. It could be any four persons that fit the criteria. I think any one of them could be fit to be with that one person. So, I don't fully believe in the whole soul mate thing. I think you have a person that's going to be perfect for you, whether that's a soul mate or not. Well, I think there's someone who's perfect for you, someone who you can live with and tolerate and it wouldn't be an issue. It wouldn't be complex to live with them or to love them, or to have a beautiful relationship.

"Thank you for sharing your journey."
You're welcome.

Still Searching For Love in All the Wrong Places

How do you know when you
Need to continue to work at it
And at what point do you throw
In the red flag, suck up your pride,
Place a lock on your heart and
Simply walk away?

When do you know you've
Compromised your spirit?

How do you know when
You need to just trust?

When do you know that you've
Given all that you can give?

How do you know when there's
Still unfinished business?

When do you know that you've
Lost your way?

How do you know that your
Heart won't break?

When do you know that
You never knew....?

How do you know when you
Need to continue to work at it
And at what point do you throw
In the red flag, suck up your pride,
Place a lock on your heart and
Simply walk away?

Signed,
Still Searching for "Love"
— Mary E. Gilder

Zack

CHAPTER SIX
Guarded

Zodiac Sign: Scorpio
Approximate Age: Forties
Occupation: Retired Military and Graphic Designer
Passions: Argentine Tango and Cooking
Hobbies: Reading and Running

"I was very guarded with my feelings to the point where I knew that I was just one of those people in the world that was just destined to be alone. They live a solitary life. They live life on their terms. They exist on whatever they have, no one to depend on but themselves, and possibly a couple of really close friends, but not on that deep of an intimate level. I believe that there's a certain understanding, a certain connection that comes with a level of intimacy that can only be brought in a relationship. But I was going to

be alone. I was going to have people in my life that would come in and out, but I was going to be alone." —Zack

"Describe your first experience with romantic love."

I got married really young. I got my girlfriend— who eventually became my wife— pregnant when I was in high school. So my first son was born when I was still in high school, and my second was born right after I joined the Navy. I believed I loved her [my girlfriend] and that's why I married her. I had a history. I had kids with this woman. We were actually married for a long time, probably longer than we should have been. The first couple of years we spent away, apart from each other. I was in the Navy so I was gone a lot. I went overseas. I went to schools. I went across the country, and then I left. I decided to leave the Navy, leave active duty. And maybe it wasn't the best decision in the world, but it was mine to make and I made it.

I started working on the base as a civilian. I didn't really have much in the way of marketable skills. I could fuel airplanes. I worked around airplanes a lot, so that kind of limited where I could work. I know that probably caused my then-wife to lose a lot of faith in me, because it was tough; it was very tough. I couldn't find a job, but I tried. I really did.

"You stated your wife loss faith in you. Could you please elaborate on that and what it did to your self-esteem?"

In regards to her losing faith, it felt like I was letting down the person who was supposed to have the most faith in me. I felt like a failure. You definitely feel like a failure, like you doubt your ability to rise to the challenge. But, you know when you wake up in the morning and it's still there, the challenge is still there— the challenge to try and make things better—yet you're kind of daunted by the possibility of failing.

For a while it was kind of demoralizing. It was like, "Oh God, this again." It's like trying really hard to do the same thing over and over again, knowing at the end of the day you're probably going to fail. You don't see victory. You don't want to win; you want to survive. There's a difference and that determines your outlook. I think for me, in my head, I was just trying to survive, and that was enough.

Anyway, I think I said eight years. During the sixth or seventh year of our marriage, I just didn't know what my options were. I didn't feel like I had options in terms of employment, aside from going back to school, but I wasn't getting that support to go to school. It was like, "You need to work. You can't go to school." Meanwhile, she had the opportunity to go to school and get a really decent job. I guess that's another story.

"Was there intimacy?"

It was just the idea that there was still the need and the wanting to have intimacy. I felt like that's all I had left. It was the kind of moment where you just connect with somebody, even if just on a physical level. I could not connect with her on any level. I got a little bit of resistance from her, and sometimes she would question my masculinity by saying stuff like, "A real man wouldn't be in this situation." It hurt. When somebody is cruel, you don't see what's inside their head. You just feel their words and you feel the hurt of the intent. You don't always understand their intent.

After our third child, the doctor said it was too dangerous to have another child because she had had three cesareans, so she had her tubes tied. Yes, they were tied. So when this next revelation occurred, I was floored. I remember the day. I can't remember the date, but I remember the day. I was getting ready to go to work and her purse was in the bathroom. I kind of knocked it over and I found a couple of packets of condoms. Oh, it hurt. It's like you know that your wife can't have children, and knowing that you're supposed to be married, in a committed relationship with her and to find the condoms... In my mind, it only meant one thing: she was having an affair. She was having an affair and apparently there was something that I wasn't doing that made her go elsewhere. And it took me a long time to even confront her about it. I was afraid of her answer. I kept it down. As a younger man I did the whole male thing. I sucked it up. That's what you're taught growing up. "Suck it up" or "Walk it off." That's it.

It hurt. It really hurt. It was like, "Here I am trying my best to fight the good fight, and trying to provide a way of life for my family. I've got three kids. I mean, a wife and three kids, and I'm failing. I had to admit it. But instead of getting the support I needed, I find out that she's looking elsewhere. My ideas about "couple hood" or "couple dom" are stated best in our marriage vows, "for better or for worse." I think a lot of people forget about that. It's like they say, "For better or for worse," but people only want to stick around for the better. When the worst comes around, it doesn't matter who, man or woman, your first instinct is to bolt and that's what she did. My wife decided to bail out on me.

I felt like I was trying my hardest to make this work— make this life with my wife and my kids work. Yet, I felt betrayed. I guess I'm kind of strange, compared to other guys, because I went around the world in the Navy and temptations were there. You know the saying, "What happens overseas, stays overseas," right? But for me, it was like no. It doesn't have to be like that. I'm married. I got this ring on my hand to remind me of my commitment to somebody. I don't know if that makes me different from any other guy, or if I'm just like the "weirdo." But I was in it for the long haul. For however long it goes, whatever relationship I've ever been in, that was my philosophy. I've had very few relationships because the relationships I've had were so long. Like I stated, "For better or worse." I don't know if that's good, bad or indifferent, but that's who I am, for better or for worse.

"Please describe how this revelation impacted your heart."

I know it was very damaging. I know near the end, before the divorce, I got very angry and it hurts to say this because I don't want people to judge. I feel like if you say stuff that notes your vulnerabilities, it makes some people feel uncomfortable. Well, I got angry and I got abusive. I know there's no excuse. I took my anger out on my sons, and I took it out on her.

"Did you confront her about your concerns?"

Well, one morning I was getting ready to go to work. Somehow we pick the most inopportune time to confront somebody about really sensitive stuff and that's just what I did. She was getting ready to leave for work or I was getting ready to leave for work and I just kind of asked her straight out, "What are condoms doing in your purse?" and she couldn't answer me. It was like, "You having an affair? Are you cheating on me? Are you having sex with somebody? What's the deal?" She couldn't answer me. A little later on, I think a day later, she actually stated that she needed to do something that would wake me up, that would shake me out of it and I thought, *If you thought or felt like I was cheating on you, that would be something.* To this day I don't know what makes me more mad. You know, whether or not she actually had an affair or she cheated on me, which I believe in my heart and soul that she did. It's like the saying in the courts, "The evidence is there." If she's fixed, and she's had her tubes tied and she can't have children, there's only one reason why she'd have condoms in her possession. Whether or not she wanted to deceive me into doing something else, I don't know what hurt more. Either one, either way, whatever happened…I felt like the bottom of my heart had just dropped out. That feeling where you're just so hurt your heart drops in your stomach? That's what I felt, both times. This is twice from the same woman, the woman I had committed myself to a life with. But at the same time, there was that whole thing, for better or for worse. I'm in it for the long haul and I wanted to make it work. But I was young and I knew that I didn't have the tools to deal with it. I just kept getting angrier and angrier and angrier, until one day I actually hit my son so hard it left a mark and she ended up calling the cops and that's when we separated. I think we were separated for about a year and then she decided to file papers.

"Describe how you felt when papers were served on you."

I was kind of relieved. Honestly, at that point, for some reason I'd been hurt. And instead of really trying, what I did was I stuck around and bottled up my anger. Yes, that's what I did. Instead of trying to confront it and trying to make it work, I sat around and just hoped that the fact of my very presence alone would fix things and it didn't.

A big part of me was relieved because I felt like I didn't want to have to work so hard for somebody who hurt me or be committed to somebody who essentially hurt me twice.

If she had said something like, "I apologize," it would have made it a tad bit better. But honestly, the truth in my head is she cheated on me. In her head the truth may be, "Oh, I did it to shake him up." I never caught her, but to me, like I said, the evidence was there.

"Was there validation of your pain from her?"

There was never "I'm sorry that I hurt you" or "I'm sorry that I made you feel like this." I was trying to make it work, yet I didn't get any validation or empathy from her. Part of me—the logical person in me and the person in me who tries to feel and tries to love—is asking, "Why the hell am I still here?"

"How did this "thing," the adultery, impact you perception of love?"

I know for a long time I was guarded. I was very guarded with my feelings to the point where I knew that I was just one of those people in the world that was just destined to be alone. They live a solitary life. They live life on their terms. They exist on whatever they have, no one to depend on but themselves, and possibly a couple of really close friends, but not on that deep of an intimate level. I believe that there's a certain understanding, a certain connection that comes with a level of intimacy that can only be brought in a relationship. But I was going to be alone. I was going to have people in my life that come in and out, but I was going to be alone. I just didn't want to get hurt.

I think it's worse for men. It's harder for men to kind of expose themselves emotionally. The secret that women don't really know or understand is that men are probably *twice* as sentimental as women. It's just we can't express it. We're taught by peer pressure, by what's thrown at us from the media, by what we're taught growing up that you can't show any sign of weakness. If you show that to another man, it's like you're just crazy. You show that to a woman, you're just weak. But the thing is that it's within us. I mean, we're human beings. We're two sides of that same coin, but there are certain things that we can't share and I think one of them is our emotions, our capacity to have emotions, to feel, not just love. We're just told we can't manifest it the same way.

"Was there a time when trust resurfaced? And if yes, what was its stimulus?"

Yes, right after the separation. Once I realized that it was over, I started connecting with somebody I worked with. I think everybody in the office saw the connection and after a while we couldn't even hide it.

"Had you healed? Were you ready to venture into something new?"

I wasn't, but I didn't realize it until we actually decided to be like a couple and live together. A year after the separation, it just kind of happened. I started dating. I probably hadn't healed. I knew I hadn't healed, but I was just trying to replace one with another. I was just trying to find a safe haven. I was tying a port in the storm, just some place to kind of be where I felt like I was loved, and I found it in Deanna.

I had very few relationships, but this one was probably the most intense and the most passionate. It was a freaking rollercoaster ride—ups and downs. She was very fiery. But looking back, I kind of realize how intense and passionate it was. It was probably not the best thing for me. But where I was, it was more like a painkiller. It was kind of there to take away the pain from being hurt the first time. She and I were a couple for three years and then after that we were kind of on and off for three years. After the first three years, I kind of got the suspicion that she was seeing somebody else. She started getting rides to work from this guy who would come and pick her up. Then when I came home one day, I was checking the messages on the machine and there was a message from the guy, and he's like telling her "da-da-dah" and then he goes, "I just want to let you know I love you." So yeah.

"How did you deal with that?"

I wasn't violent. I was upset and I was pissed, but I found myself in the very same position I had been in before. I found my heart dropping to my stomach again and I moved out of the house and back in with my parents. Family is always my safe haven.

I'd come to find out a couple weeks later, about a month later, that the guy she was dating was cheating on his wife, and he ended it [with Deanna] about a month later when he decided to go back to his wife. I kind of knew that because she called me just before it happened and said, "I don't know what's going on." She came back to me, to lean on me, and I told myself that I should have just hung up when she called, but no. Again, I felt like I'm in it for the long haul, for better or for worse, you know? I was going to be a friend for her, which was probably not the best thing in the world, but there I was.

"Did your value system play into this? And if yes, how?"

It's just you don't want to walk away. You don't abandon friends. You don't abandon people you love. Well, the guy ended up leaving her, and we had a kind of on-again off-again relationship. We weren't really lovers, but we were more than friends. And that lasted another three years. She would go out on dates and I would get jealous, and I wouldn't say anything. But, at the end of those three years, I realized I couldn't take it anymore. I wanted to be with somebody exclusively and I wanted to be in that relationship. Part of me decided to stand up for myself. It's like, "You know what? I can't take this anymore. It's either this or that." Maybe that's not fair, but that's who I am. And I said, "You know what? I'm not sure I can do this on-again off-again relationship."

"What impact did this relationship have on your self-esteem?"

At that point, what self-esteem? It's like this person was in my life and because of what happened before this person was in my life, I was living for that moment—the moment that I had her, the moment that she was there, the moment I was holding her, the moment that we were together.

That's not the basis for a long-term relationship, where you're just so much living for the moment that you're not thinking about the next day, the next month, the next year or the next ten years. You're just happy that you have her now. You have this tenuous feeling like it's all about endings. You feel like you enjoy the moment because a minute from now it could all just go away. It could be dust in my hand. Nothing. When you're in a relationship that you're committed to, that's not a way to live. That's not the kind of feeling you want to have. You want to be able to wake up in the morning next to that person knowing that if they were to disappear, that they were with you. They were committed to being with you for life. Anything else, you might as well be walking on a glass bridge. You know, just a fiberglass bridge. Anyway, I'd gotten to that point in the second half of our relationship where she had complete control over my heart.

Mary, at that point she was my addiction. You get to that point where your self-esteem is so low, it's like you just want that person. At the same time, it's very tenuous because you can't count on the next day. But that's where I was. I didn't see it for what it was. Part of me wanted to make it work, but I needed to leave, but I wanted to settle things. I actually loved this person. I loved her with all my heart, even with all the things she did— all the dating, all of the cheating. I loved her. We were so intense. We would be at each other's throats one minute and having hot, sweaty, passionate sex the next. I knew that the relationship was not good for me, but it was so intense that it was just a rush just being in it. It might have been (an addiction). It's like, "Oh, man," and "God, she drives me crazy." It's great for like a rollercoaster, but for a long-term relationship, it's probably not healthy. But I knew near the end, she was starting to get detached. I knew something was going on. I said, "We've been together for six years on and off, I love you. I want more. I want a life with you."

That's when she stated, "I met somebody two weeks ago and he's from Washington State and he asked me to marry him."

One more time, my heart drops into my stomach and my world falls apart again. That was ten years ago, because I'd just turned thirty. I'm forty-two now. But I know for about ten or eleven years, I refrained from even looking for relationships. I was hurt. I really had no confidence in my ability to be in a relationship, knowing that I'd been hurt twice. I'd went back to that whole mindset of, "There are some people in the world that are meant to be alone and I am one of them." You can kind of get yourself in the mindset where you believe it, but it doesn't make the pain feel any better. And in more ways, it hurts. But at the same time, I knew that I wasn't going to get hurt anymore. So, I went out with friends. I did everything but date somebody. I probably robbed myself of the opportunity for probably some very meaningful relationships because of my fear, my foreboding fear that it would eventually lead to me getting hurt. I refrained.

"Has personal growth manifested in this area?"

Near the end when I actually started dating and I actually met somebody, I realized that I hadn't forgiven myself, which is a big thing. No matter who's at fault, you must forgive yourself in order to forgive the other person. I felt like, "Yeah, you hurt me. You ripped my heart out of my lungs and you showed it to me while it was still beating, but yet I forgive you." If you don't do that, if you don't resolve those feelings, if you don't put them to rest, you're stuck there. You're trapped. You're chained to that point in your life and you're not going to move forward. And that's what I needed to do—move forward.

I recall reflecting on why I seemed to end up with women that hurt me. I really thought about it because I know that looking back, and knowing who these women are now...

they say that hindsight is 20/20. The farther away you get from things, the more objective you can become.

Silence.

You know what? I was a nice guy. I've been told that repeatedly. I would like to think that's true because that's something I'm pretty proud of, you know? I'm a nice guy, but for both of these women it wasn't enough. They wanted something more. My ex-wife wanted someone that would give her a life that she would like to be accustomed to. Deanna wanted to have the family, the marriage, the child, the building the life together, which I was perfectly happy to give to her. If she would've asked me, I would have said yes. But looking back, I didn't say that to her. I never stated that I would like that kind of life too. In my defense, she never asked me. She never said, "Hey, this is what I want from a relationship and you're just not fulfilling it."

In regards to insecurity and emotional capacity during the second relationship, I know I gave to her all I had. Whether or not that was enough, whether or not that was either 50% and I was protecting the rest, or 30% and I was protecting the rest, I know, looking back, that I gave her all I had. Is that enough? Only she can say that. But I believe that I gave my all to it.

"Have you opened your heart to possibilities? The possibility of someone entering your life after these two relationships?"

First, I must say that ten years passed before I started dating again. And when I resumed dating, it was somebody completely out of the blue, somebody I worked with. I had a couple of relationships that were kind of failure to launch. They never went anywhere. But this one person I dated, she was twenty-two. I was forty-one or forty-two. I think it was the idea of having a younger woman, a way younger woman in my life; maybe the shock value or having somebody there who actually liked me. But as it got farther along, I kind of realized that she was young. She was twenty-two, but I felt like I was dealing with a teenager and all the head games she would play drove me crazy. I realized as soon as I walked away from that one that, "You know what? It's not always you." Women can be just as screwed up. They do some of the same things. In the 21st century, they play some of the same games that only men played in the 20th century. It's no-holds-barred. It's equal opportunity hurt, okay? It's like they can play the games. The game is on. I can do these things. I can play the head games and I came to realize, with age comes wisdom and realizing that there's always the other half of the equation. There's always that other side of the story and that it's not always you.

The second relationship that I was in, I think I said I gave all I had, whether that was 100% or 50%. I was holding back and just saving that. I gave all I felt I had to give.

So we also had talked about these 'starter dates' that I had. I dated a twenty-two-year-old and after a couple of months, I realized it wasn't just me. I realized women will play games and, in some cases, they can afford to be worse at it. They can afford to kind of play no-holds-barred and not hold anything back. I think a lot of women do this. This may be a grossly broad generalization, but I think a lot of women realize that when this guy is gone, they can get another one. They see us as easy to replace. Whether or not that's true or not for most women or any woman, I could be wrong, but that's what I see. I see it in the women I hang out with.

I was talking to this one coworker. She talked about seeing one guy while she was dating another, and I said, "Well, how do you know that the guy that you're cheating on, isn't the one?" You're trying to base the possibility of a lifetime with someone just on a few weeks, or a day or an hour. Cultivating a relationship like that takes a lot of time and a lot of emotional investment. Not to make it sound business-like, but you know, it takes an investment. It takes you putting yourself into that and them doing the same.

"Do you believe that women wear masks as a counter to the masks men wear?"

It could be. That might be true, especially in the times that we live in now because image is everything. How we present ourselves to others means more than real character sometimes, so that could be true, especially now. If it is, it's a sad thing. It's just a really sad thing because if that's all we do and that's all we present, then we're shortchanging that person who's across from us and we're shortchanging ourselves because we're not allowing ourselves the full experience of a really truthful and honest relationship.

Like I said, I'm in my forties and it's not that I have all of the answers. It's just I'm starting to realize what questions to ask to get those answers. I don't know everything. I don't claim to know everything. I just know what life has given to me and that is rich experiences.

I was just reflecting on the twenty-two-year-old. Mary, she played games and then broke up with me and then tried to get back into my life. Then she started dating somebody else and we were still working together. She even called after we had broken up and after I'd kind of decided to move on. She called saying, "You know, I don't want you to talk about our relationship with anybody."

At first I asked, "Why would I do that in the first place?" What's done is done. You know? Then I kind of led her on. I was like, "I was in a committed relationship. I loved you for better or for worse. I loved you and then you broke up with me." I basically unloaded. I did this big unloading about how I felt and how it made me feel when she broke up with me. "Now, you present me with this?"

She goes, "Well, you know you have this reputation…" It's like, "Okay?"

I turned something that she said about herself against her. I go, "Well, why do you even care? You're the one who said you don't care what other people think. Why should it even bother you?"

At that moment I thought, *I don't need this. I need to move forward.* It's like one of those moments when you realize you're stuck in that moment and you're just keeping yourself chained to the moment because that's all you have. At the same time, you're not moving forward; you're just stuck. I realized at that time that I needed to move forward. It was easy. It was easier than I thought it would be to kind of walk away. I don't know if it was because I had kind of grown up or if I was just being heartless about the whole thing, just being a regular guy. I don't know. All I know is that it wasn't all my fault and I could walk away from this with my dignity and my sanity intact. It was kind of liberating at a certain point. It was like, "Man, okay. This is okay. It's not all me. I'm not completely at fault. I'm not a terrible person."

"Can you provide more depth as it pertains to the liberation you identified with and how that impacted your self-esteem?"

Can I be honest with you? Seriously, you know what? At that point, she was so inexperienced. But honestly, I think that in my eyes, the fact that I was having sex with a twenty-two-year-old, was more appealing than the actual act. And I'll tell you why. The idea of having sex with a twenty-two-year-old is cool. It's great. It brings up your street cred. If you're a younger man, your friends are like, "Yeah." But I think at that point I was dating somebody who really didn't have much of a life experience. She was twenty-two and kind of sheltered. It was okay, though. It was just a younger body, you know? It doesn't really have the experience to really explore a sexual life. I'm not saying I really get into freaks. That's not the point. The point is somebody is willing to experiment, someone who brings stuff to that. I think for that reason, I actually prefer older women. For a long time I have preferred older women. [When dating the twenty-two year old,] I went so against my preferences because I needed to. I needed to kind of go the other way, if only temporarily, if only maybe for a couple of times. But my preferences put into my mind the clear cut things I needed in my head of what I was looking for in a partner. I was looking for somebody who was a lot more mature, a lot more experienced, life experienced. Because in order for a "better or worse" type relationship [to succeed], you need somebody who can play that mature role. Because in relationships you play roles. You assume a role because that's what you need to do. For example, when your partner in a relationship gets depressed or she gets fired or something happens to her, you have to be the father figure. You have to be the caregiver. You have to be the person who gives her comfort. That's an example. And it works both ways. You fulfill certain roles in each other's lives, not because you have to but because you've committed yourself to it and you want to. So, I don't think the person I was dating had the breadth of experience to be able to do that for me. It was more like a one-sided relationship; I could do that for her, but the other way around? Forget it. It was not gonna happen. I think also the fact that she kind of broke up with me around the time that my dad died, that might have a lot to do with it. My dad passed away from cancer, after a long battle, and the breakup happened around the same time.

So where were we? The twenty-two-year-old was over with. Actually, that was a pretty tumultuous time in my life. I was just trashed emotionally because my dad had passed away, and I watched him kind of fade away one piece at a time. To just slowly see this man who raised me kind of slowly deteriorate, to see the strength leave a man day by day slowly broke my heart. The fact that the twenty-two-year-old was immature enough to break up with me while my dad was going through all this, I think gave me the opportunity to realize, "Hey, I'm not so screwed up. I'm okay. I can bring something to a mature relationship." So, this is about the time I met my current girlfriend whose name is Kelli.

Three months after my dad passed away, at a friend's urging I started taking up dancing. I danced the Argentine Tango. It's a very intimate, very passionate dance. I think it was something that kind of allowed me to express myself in a way I'd never done before. It was also a great way to meet women, right? So I met Kelli. You learn to dance, and you just perform these performances. You actually go to nightclubs where they have these parties called "Milongas" and you dance socially. You go to a place and you dance with people and the objective is not to pick up; it's to form a connection with someone on the dance floor and it could be with somebody who's married somebody who's dating, or somebody who's single. The idea is to connect with somebody on this level. I met Kelli. We'd taken some classes together and for some reason we connected.

We'd dance with each other, but we wouldn't dance with each other exclusively. We'd save a couple dances for each other. I loved our waltzes together; I saved my waltzes for Kelli. I think it was about a year and a half after we started going out. I mean, not like dating but like going out and saying, "Okay, I'll go to this one [Milonga], if you go." We kind of would go as a couple, but kind of a non-couple, though, because it's really intimidating to go in by yourself, so we'd go together. We were friends daring each other. "Well, I'll go to this class, but you must go to this dance with me." So, I was on my best behavior the entire time. I was a gentleman, a perfect gentleman. I had to share this because it's such a cool story. Anyway, one night we were driving home from a San Francisco Milonga and I was taking her home to her house and she had said, "Zack, you've been a really nice guy. You're really nice and fun to be around. And you've been a gentleman. You've treated me like no other person I've dated so far but," and she grabbed my hand and she goes, "I'd really like you to misbehave more." So that began our relationship. It's been about a year now.

"What strengths do you bring to this relationship? What makes this one a good fit for you?"

I ask myself this question often and have concluded that I'm just not taking myself too seriously. Every time I make a mistake, I now understand that it's not the end of the world. I think that has a lot to do with the past. I used to be so hard on myself that I couldn't really go on. I don't know if that makes sense. Like when you're so down on yourself when you make even a minor mistake, you just want to give up because you just made a mistake and you're saying to yourself, *Oh I'm terrible at this and I don't want to do it again.* But I realized during the ten years that I was not alone, I was being way too hard on myself. I needed to lighten up and forgive the people who hurt me in my life, and even more important I needed to forgive myself. I think that's a big part of it. I had never forgiven myself. I had just basically said, "It's over. You're terrible. You're just going to be alone because you deserve to be alone."

"Do you feel joy in this relationship?"

Yeah. I don't know if it's joy or just true love or whatever. I don't know if joy means you just like waking up with the person you're with in the morning. When you wake up in the morning and it's like, "Yeah, I just want to be here." She could do something, I could be mad at her or she could be mad at me, but I'm not going to bail. I love this person enough to know that thing that she does, that's only temporary. That's just a speed bump in life, you know? Just move on. You move forward. It's like, "I still want to be part of it. I still like this person who's in front of me. I still appreciate and adore this person who's in front of me. And I'm pretty certain it's mutual."

"How do you know it's mutual?"

The way she says *sweetheart* when she talks to me. The way she brings to my attention that what I'm eating has too much salt and I have to look out for my blood pressure. The way she still lets me go dance tango, even though she's hurt her back and she hasn't been able to do it for months. I realize that's something that brings me a certain level of fulfillment, the way that I can ask her to do something. I can ask her a favor and know that she would do it, even though I probably wouldn't want her to do it because I'm too proud.

I would do anything she would ask me to. The fact that she realizes that we both need our space, and there's an understanding of each other as people, as individuals. We both acknowledge that other person on the other side. Also, we both understand that there is still something we can learn from each other. I bring certain things to this relationship that maybe she doesn't have that I can teach her.

"Please give an example of something you can teach, wisdom that you can provide."

I often provide wisdom as it pertains to men and their ability to love. I say patience because a lot of the time being men, we're kind of grabbed by the physical and the visual. We're so enamored with the shell or the mask that we talked about earlier, that we're so distracted by that and we don't really understand or know the real person that's inside. I think a good relationship requires patience because a good relationship requires a long time to cultivate to make it good. It's like raising a child or raising plants or something that is a commitment, to be there and to be willing to be there for the bad as well as the good. Because if you're only around for the good parts, and you bail during the bad parts, then you've robbed yourself of half of the experience. The more you as a couple experience the entire relationship, the better it will be. If you experience the worst, it makes you appreciate the best parts even more because you know how bad it can get.

"Do you believe that men have the capacity to love deeply?"

Men can get hurt so badly that it will get in the way of them giving themselves the opportunity to love fully and deeply. But then they shield it by acting like an ass or being aloof. I got hurt so badly and for a long period of time I felt that there was no hope. It was over. I was damaged. I was damaged goods. I was a totaled car. Even more so, we can be so damaged that we become afraid to show the depth of our vulnerability to other people.

"How do you feel a man's vulnerability is processed by women?"

If a man surrenders his vulnerability, some women in turn will believe that he doesn't have what it takes to be in a relationship because he's so easily hurt or so deeply hurt and that he's weak. I think we're afraid to show vulnerability because we equate vulnerability with weakness. And in our minds, that's not something we want to exhibit to women.

"Do you believe that a man can love from the depths of his soul?"

Yes. I mean, I think if we didn't believe that, we wouldn't be trying to be in relationships. Most guys, not the guys that are just there for the playing, but just the everyday guy who's just looking for somebody to love. I think if you don't have the opportunity to drink deeply from the well, what's the point?

"Do you believe that the adulterer and the playboy are simply searching for love?"

Yeah. I mean, the person who keeps going back to the bottle, who drinks, the person who goes back to drugs, the person who cheats incessantly, man or woman, you know anybody...they're obviously looking for something. There is a void in their life that they're trying to fill. I think what it is they're not working on quality; they're just working on quantity. It could be they're still looking, but they're so not into wanting to see the other person, especially adulterous people who date a lot of people at the same time. They're going after the façade and once they escape the façade, they realize that's not what they wanted and they go on to the next one. It's a constant audition process for the right one.

Going back to what I said, cultivating that relationship requires patience, patience to pull back those layers of the shell of the façade. It took a long time for us to decide that we were dating, and it just felt right when it did happen. But yes, the adulterer is definitely looking for somebody, for acceptance to fill a void.

"In closing, how did you know that your soul had been touched? At what point did you know that it was safe to pull back the layers and reveal your heart?"

Mary, I knew because I wanted to commit myself to her. I pulled back the layers. I broke open my shell and made an incredible leap of faith. I stepped out on faith because I believe in love.

"Thank you for trusting me with your words."

Turned out to be a great experience.

Love is Me

How someone could "LOVE" so much and has yet to ever fall in LOVE, "True LOVE not lust or infatuation". How does one know the feeling and has yet to understand the true meaning. What is LOVE? I ponder to myself while seeking the answer to this question and realize that I'm LOVE. I LOVE myself unconditionally; I know how it feels to LOVE deeply because I LOVE myself spiritually. My LOVE is pure! I LOVE "LOVE" and that LOVE is "ME" I fell in LOVE, true LOVE~ —CheyNaRey

Brion

CHAPTER SEVEN
Didn't Give A Fuck

Zodiac Sign: Libra
Approximate Age: Thirties
Occupation: Self Employed
Passions: Music, Football, Poetry,
Volunteering and Sports
Hobbies: Writing Screen Plays,
Dominos and Creating Music

"When she walked out, I had the I-don't-care attitude. I really didn't care about anything. My mother likes to call it, "I don't give a FUCK" attitude. I took that attitude wherever I went and it started to haunt me. I moved around from place to place and treated people differently. I got into a couple relationships; one that started off very wrong because I was just looking for somebody to be with, not

necessarily somebody to love. I just wanted somebody who would accept me for who I was, but at that point I wasn't myself. I was somebody else and I failed to realize that. That somebody else was very dysfunctional, but I was thinking that I was myself.

For those people that knew me and the people who didn't, they all saw what I didn't. They all saw pure ugliness. I was just angry. I felt like I could do whatever I wanted to. If you told me to go left, I'd go right and to the middle just to show you that I wasn't going left. I just wasn't a person that you wanted to be around. I exerted negativity. I didn't want to do anything productive or positive." —Brion

"At a young age, what were your thoughts as they pertained to love?"

From whatever age I could talk until age eighteen, my perception of love was kind of disguised or it was kind of masked because I did not have both parents there to show me what real love was supposed to be. My parents divorced when I was five years old. Pops was married but wanted to live the single playboy life on the side. He was a professional man; graduated from college and could talk the talk. He had a bad addiction and that was young women. Growing up, I never understood why because my mom was young, educated and very beautiful. She made it her priority to meet his needs because that's how she is, putting her man first. But I guess he wasn't satisfied with that.

I got a perception from my mom of what love was supposed to be just because she loved me unconditionally. She loved other people unconditionally and taught me the importance of that. Not having my father around kind of shifted me into different directions. I didn't really know how to show a woman love because, you know, my father wasn't there to make an example or show me the example of how to do that. So I kind of had to teach myself. I had a lot of help along the way, though, just with family and relatives being around that were in full-functioning relationships. Simple things, for example, like giving your woman a massage or telling her she looks nice, or different things like that, I kind of learned from elsewhere, instead of in my home, because I didn't have that around.

"What were some of the positive things you learned?"

All right, some of the positive things I learned from the men in my life; first of all, be responsible. I think being responsible is like a key thing to being at least a 90% man. You need to be responsible in the things that you do, or responsible for the things that you do whether they're positive or negative, anything of that sort. Also, just being up-front, being very forward with people, and being a "stand-up man." You have to always be honest with people. Nowadays, people at any point in the juncture are going to judge you based on what kind of person you present yourself to be. Whether you're honest, whether you're dishonest or whether you have a degree of intelligence. That's what I learned from the males in my life. Unfortunately, I had to learn mistakes from the males in my life also. From my father, I had to learn that you have to be responsible. Now that could go either negative or positive. My father wasn't responsible enough to take care of his responsibility, which was me and eight other kids that he had. He bounced around from woman to woman, you know, just real foul, not honest or trustworthy at all. So like I said before, learning in a positive manner, it's the same thing that I learned in a negative manner.

Now moving forward to my stepfather; he was also very positive in me becoming a man. He was a positive role model because he taught me how to be responsible for myself. "Forget what everybody else is doing. Don't worry about what everybody else is doing. Just worry about yourself and you will be able to complete the whole battle if you worry about yourself." With that said, there were decisions my step-father made that I did not agree with but that's life. But as you grow older, you learn to grow from that and not hold people accountable for that. You just let things go. Sometimes you got to let things go. I would like to thank both of those people, my father and my stepfather. My father passed away, and my stepfather is still alive and well. My stepfather and I have a good relationship. He and my mother are still together, and I would like to thank both of them for that, because I feel like it has made me 100%.

"Describe your first experience with love."

The first time I felt love come over me, or [the first time I was] led to being in love, it was about 2001. I was working at Target. I met this girl. I was working with her at the time. At first I was real flirty with her, but one day I came to work and realized that I was nervous. I've never been nervous to do anything, I mean, I do music. I've been in plays. I've even done screenings for commercials and I was never nervous. But I came to work that one day nervous as hell and I was trying to figure out why. I saw this young lady that I'm talking about and I had butterflies in my stomach, and I couldn't even talk to her. I started to question myself, like, "What's wrong with me?" I had to say, "Self! Self, are you listening? What is going on? Why can't you muster up any words to talk?" Later on, probably about a week after this happened, I realized that I was in love with this person and that wasn't the first thing that came across my mind. I just felt like I was having a weird day. Something came over me, like a weird feeling. It felt good, though. And now I still get those same feelings because I'm still with this person.

So with me being with this person, there are times that I plan things for her, dates so that she can go get her manicure, pedicure, whatever. I try to set aside time where she can have time with herself and be with her friends and pamper herself. But at the same time, I know that she's being pampered on my account and that leaves me with a smile on my face.

All right, when this relationship first began, everything was beautiful. I felt like I was on top of the world. I had the woman that I wanted. She had a daughter who was five years old at the time. She was amazing. She just like gravitated toward me. I loved her just like she was my biological child. We [me and her mother] spent every moment together, pretty much. When I wasn't with her, I was doing whatever I had to do, work, whatever, but I was mostly around them. They were my family. After two years of being together, I asked her to marry me. I proposed to her and she said yes. Everything was what I would describe as perfect.

Whenever I was around this woman, I felt amazing. I didn't want for anything. I didn't want for anyone else. I didn't feel like I needed to go anywhere for anything. She captivated my mind, heart and soul. I can't even describe the words that you would use to describe a 100% woman, but she made me feel like a 100% man. I'm talking about everything from conversation to love making, to just our personalities. We were just open with each other. We could say anything, do anything together, without being embarrassed. We could say goofy stuff, say whatever the heck we wanted off the top of our head. I didn't feel like I was being judged or criticized for what I would say or do, and that was something new to me because I had never had anything like that before. I think likewise, she felt the same way, because everything was just there. Everything was 100%. We just went together like, what Forest Gump say? Peas and carrots. That's how we went together.

So, moving forward, we're still in this relationship. We were scheduled to have a wedding and at this time I was in the Marine Corp. At this point something had gone wrong. My father had died. I didn't spend a lot of time with my father, but I spent his last moments with him. So, it had a lot of effect on my mental state, how I perceived a lot of things. After my father died, I reported back to my duty station on the East Coast and nothing was the same anymore. I went back to the military. I felt cheated of the chance to sit with him, not as father and son but as man to man and look him in the eyes and ask why! Why did you marry my mother? Why did you disrespect her? Why did you father nine children and not provide for any of them? I would want to know how he could walk away from a marriage and turn his back on his responsibility. I needed to know what was done to him as a child to make him this way. I needed to know if he had a heart, if he had a soul. But more importantly, I wanted him to know that I forgave him and I felt cheated out of the opportunity to have that closure. I just became an angry person. I don't know why. It may have been because I never had that time with my father and I always thought he would be around, so we could get that time back, but we didn't.

I left the military. I was discharged and that kind of destroyed everything that me and this woman had together because I lied to her. I made her believe that I was going back. I didn't open up and tell her what really happened and that I wasn't going back and that I didn't feel the same. I didn't want to do this anymore. I didn't want to live the kind of lifestyle that I was living. I didn't want to be in the situation that I was in. I just became angry with everybody. It got to a point where me and her would fight. I mean, we had our little incidents here and there, but I got to the point where I would be yelling full steam at her a lot, and she got tired of it and she left. That was it.

"Her walking away, what did that feel like?"

All right, when she walked out, I had the I-don't-care attitude. I really didn't care about anything. My mom likes to call it the I-don't-give-a-fuck attitude. I took that attitude wherever I went and it started to haunt me. I moved around from place to place and treated people differently. I got into a couple relationships; one that started off very wrong because I was just looking for somebody to be with, not necessarily somebody to love. I just wanted somebody who would accept me for who I was, but at that point I wasn't myself. I was somebody else and I failed to realize that. That somebody else was very dysfunctional, but I was thinking that I was myself.

For those people that knew me and the people who didn't, they all saw what I didn't. They all saw pure ugliness. I was just angry. I felt like I could do whatever I wanted to. If you told me to go left, I'd go right and to the middle just to show you that I wasn't going left. I just wasn't a person that you wanted to be around. I exerted negativity. I didn't want to do anything productive or positive.

"Describe what your exertion of negativity looked like."

When I say that I exerted negativity, what I'm saying is that I did things that you wouldn't want your child to do, you wouldn't want your child to be around. For instance, I got with this one chick. We were an item, but we did real foul things together. We would set people up through money schemes. We were just like what you would call Bonnie and Clyde. We would go out, she would go and set people up and take them to hotels. We set them up like we were running a prostitution thing, setting them up and taking their money. Not to mention we were on drugs. I mean, hard drugs; crystal meth to be exact. So this dysfunctional lifestyle change made me an even angrier person because I knew I didn't want to be in that situation, but I felt like that was the only thing that was there for me. She was the only person that was there for me. I didn't have my mother because I chose not to. I didn't have my three sisters or my brother because I chose not to. I felt like I could do everything on my own, and it hurt me on the inside because when I looked in the mirror every day, I saw this person that I was becoming. I was at a very low point and I knew that was not me. I knew that was not the type of person my mother raised me to be. I knew that that wasn't the person my family knew me to be, so I never put my burdens on my family. I felt like they were burdens and they were just simple mistakes that I could have gotten myself out of from the beginning.

That led to me eventually getting this girl pregnant. We just hooked up and did drugs together. Her pregnancy motivated me not to do drugs anymore, to try and get my life right because I knew that I had this child coming and I didn't want this child to come into the world without his father being responsible. At one point, she said she would stop doing drugs, but shortly after our conversation I found needles and drugs in our house and I beat her up. I beat her up bad. I again felt like, "What am I doing here with this person?" She pissed me off to the fullest extent, so when I was in the act of putting my hands on her, I didn't care. I didn't care what became of it afterwards. I didn't care if I went to jail. I didn't care if somebody came in and beat the mess out of me. I wanted to get my point across that you are not about to bring a baby into this world that is on drugs. I was a sad case because I didn't realize that beating on her could have killed my child. I didn't think about that at that time. I just felt like I needed to get my point across. I think that's when pure evil had set in and I had no control of myself afterwards.

So after this incident, the police were called and I went to jail. This is where I hit rock bottom.

"Share with me what rock bottom was for you."

I had nobody to turn to. I had basically disowned my family. I hadn't talked to my family in probably like two years and when I did, it was because I needed something. I had nobody. I didn't even have my dysfunctional "girlfriend." I thought I was being a man, building myself up to be this man, but I wasn't because I was putting my hands on her. At one point I was a druggie, so what kind of man was I? To move on, from that I felt as though I needed to do a reevaluation of myself.

So we're now in jail; not *we* but me. At this point, I got like a whole range of emotions going on in my head and in my soul. First thing I was thinking was, "How in the hell did I wind up here?" I mean, through all of my life I had never been in trouble. Maybe I got in trouble once for being drunk in public and spent the night in detox, but I had never sat up in jail for a period of time, going to court and doing all this other stuff. This was all very new to me. My time spent in jail was very confrontational because I was forced to confront my demons. I wasn't really scared of anybody or worried about anything happening to me in there. It was just the fact of "How long am I going to be in here? And how long is it going to take for me to fight this case?" I just wanted to get out. I just wanted to be free. I was behind walls. I couldn't see outside. When I would go in the yard, the yard was indoors and it had two windows, so I could look up and all I could see was the sky. I felt so trapped. I have never felt so trapped in my life. I have never felt so claustrophobic in my life. I felt like everything was caving in on me. I was emotionally suffocating. Most nights, I cried to myself because I knew this wasn't the person that my mom raised me to be. I knew that I wasn't myself.

I knew that for me to not be behind those walls and for me to not feel trapped, I knew I had to make changes. I knew I had to make changes within myself. I had to get rid of the I-don't-give-a-fuck mentality. Actually, I needed to give a fuck. The last three months of my nine-month sentence was focused on just that. I started to make changes. It all started with my appearance. Every day I made sure that I was clean and fresh. People would say, "Dang, you're in jail. Why are you so fresh?" *Because I'm preparing myself for what's going to happen when I get out and it all starts inside.* I had to decide if I was going to be the same person that I was when I went in or was I going to be the person my mother raised? I made the choice that I was going to be the person that would make my family proud. I was going to be that person and I wanted to be that person when I got out. That meant I had to get back in touch with my family, the people that really had my back, and start being more family-oriented. I needed to regain their trust and regain their support because without a support system, you're pretty much nothing. You could do bad all by yourself, but does anyone really want to do bad by their self? I don't think so.

"It sounds as though you were creating a plan of action."

Yes, absolutely. I actually had to write it down while I was in jail. First of all, I knew that things were bad with our economy, so I needed to go to school. So the first thing that I needed to do was get a job because I had no support system to put me through school. So, I had to find a job, one that was going to stick and was going to help me so that I could go to school and just get myself in the swing of everyday living instead of doing all of the negative stuff that I had been doing— all the hustlin' and bustlin' and being in the streets and not having any focus.

When I got out, I had a couple of numbers that I had kept. I called one of my friends. He was actually living in L.A. I wasn't in L.A when all of this happened and luckily he had a job opening, and then it was kind of like scheduling myself to get out to L.A. How was I going to do that? I worked odd jobs. I worked in trenches. I dug trenches. I worked at construction sites and I worked at military construction sites. I did all kinds of odd jobs, under the table money, and I just stacked up my money, and ended up getting a Greyhound ticket and came back to L.A. I knew that I had to come first. I knew that for me to be in the right state of mind, I needed to be home. And the fact that I was away from my family was part of the problem because I had no one to turn to. I was away from that strong support system and that unconditional love that comes from an extended family foundation. So, I just did whatever so I could get back home. I started working for this carpet company and I was there seven days a week at times, working in a warehouse, driving a forklift and making good money. So, with that, a couple of months later I started looking into what kind of programs I could get into for school. I found a radiology program, and I felt like I've always wanted to work in a hospital setting, but I never had the means and the ambition to go for it. I felt like now was the proper time to do that, since everything was coming around. I had just got off probation. Everything was starting to clear up for me and I felt like school was the thing that was going to get my mind right. So what I did was I started going to school. I was working and then I got laid off at my job. What happens when you start to try and do something positive and something negative happens? I think now, looking back, or not even looking back, I knew then that it was a test. *What are you going to do, Brion? Are you going to go back to the negativity because things aren't going right for you? Or are you going to stick with the plan and remain focused and do what you have to do to get yourself right?*

In between that time, I was back in L.A. and getting used to things. Everything was going great for me. I went out to get something to eat at California Pizza Kitchen. Once I was done ordering my food, my ex-girlfriend from when I had left, my first love, appears from out of the bathroom.

"Describe what that very moment felt like."

My first love appears and even though I was with somebody else, I always held her in my heart, very close to my heart. She was always there. I always wondered what she was doing, where she was going, just what she was up to the whole time while I was gone. And then there she was, right in front of my face. I was ecstatic, like my head touched the clouds. That's how I felt. I felt like I was high, but I wasn't high on any kind of drug. This was better than any kind of drug I had ever taken into my system. And I knew that I was blessed to be with my true love.

So, there we were, standing in the restaurant catching up. She's telling me what she'd been up to and I was telling her what I'd been going through. I didn't really get into a long story because she had to get back to work, so we exchanged numbers. She was real welcoming, which was a surprise to me. I think that all of the time that had gone by gave her time to heal from what I had put her through. It wasn't like we automatically got back together, but at least I knew that there was a chance because she didn't just blow me off. She gave me her number, which meant that there was an opening for a new beginning. So little by little, I started coming back around. I started hanging out with her daughter a lot more, just kind of getting back into the mode of where I was at before but not fully there.

The two of us being at the restaurant at that very moment, exchanging numbers and talking on the phone; those were my moments of clarity. I felt like I was a brand-new person.

All that stuff that had happened to me before when I was in another state, it just kind of melted away like it never happened. It felt like I was in a state of euphoria. This, like I said, was the most gratifying thing that had happened to me in a long time. I hadn't felt this way since we were first together. And for time to have gone by and for me to feel this way, even after that time had gone away, made me feel like this was the real deal and I couldn't make any more mistakes. I couldn't give this woman up for anything in the world. I feel like every time I tell this story to somebody it still makes me want to cry. It still makes me feel how I felt when I first looked into her eyes, like when I first met her. I feel the same way—nervous, butterflies, everything, which lets me know that I'm still in love with this woman and that I have to do everything in my power to keep her.

"In your opinion, do men have the capacity to love deeply?"

Do men have the capacity to love deeply? In my opinion, of course they do. Men are human just like women are human. Just because women show it in a different way, doesn't mean that a man doesn't love as deeply. There are all sorts of ways to express your love to somebody. I think just being the opposite sex, we show it in different ways. In a lot of ways it can be misconstrued into men not having the capacity to love as deeply as women. But I definitely think that a man can love as deeply as a woman. The reason why I feel like some men can't show, or don't show, that they can love deeply is because of how they grew up.

Maybe women need to do a love background check when you meet a man. You have to do a background check on everybody because a lot of people grow up in households where they're not shown any love. It doesn't mean that they can't love deeply; it's just that in those early years when they were growing into adulthood something went drastically wrong. It's not up to us to judge or to tell what went wrong. I just feel like you have to accept that person for who they are and try to get it out of them, but not force it out. Love them the way you would want to be loved, and maybe they'll show it the same way to you.

I have an acronym for love— Lots of Volatile Emotions. You have to take into account other people's emotions when you love somebody because one of the ultimate emotions is love, so you have to be able to dish it out as well as take it in. Love, to me, is not something you throw around. It's not just a word to me. When I was at a young age, it was very rare that I was loved from a male and female perspective. I was only loved from a female perspective. But once you mix the two, it makes everything 1200% and you have to embody that full-on emotion. If you don't, you don't have it. There's plenty of ways to gain it, but you have to accept it first before you can give it. That's what love means to me.

"In your opinion, can a man have a broken heart?"

Can a man have a broken heart? Yes, he can. In my case my heart was even shattered, but it's what you do with the broken heart. Do you allow it to remain broken? Or do you pull all the pieces together and make it an unbroken heart? Anyone can have a broken heart—man, woman, child; it just depends on what that person has been through. I've been through a lot. My heart's been broken a couple of times. Like I said, it's even been shattered. But I definitely believe a man can have a broken heart. So, women, take notice. Don't think that it all revolves around you because your man, whether he shows it or not, hurts just as deeply as you and loves just as profoundly.

"Thank you for allowing me in."

Thank you, Mary.

CLOSING MESSAGE

❖

$\mathscr{I}$t is my hope that, Even a Man Can Have a Broken Heart, left each reader enlightened, empowered, encouraged and inspired. Most of all, I pray that you were challenged to reexamine your perceptions as they pertain to men and how they love.

In addition, I would like to set aside time and extend my deepest appreciation to the men: Drayke, Zayven, Brion, Zack, and Ethan for sharing with the masses a moment within your journey. It takes a great deal of courage to open your soul so that intern, others can be inspired to re assess their journey.

We all have a story, skeletons in the closet and experiences that may no longer define who we are within this moment because life happens and causes a shift on various levels. And it is my hope that as you continue your journey, these shifts push your evolution into the individual you were sent here to become.

I wish you endless love, joy, peace, passion and courage,

Mary E. Gilder-author

Even a Man Can Have a Broken Heart

By Mary Gilder

ABOUT THE GUIDE

The suggested questions should be utilized as a tool to help faciliate thought provoking group discsussions.

DISCUSSION QUESTIONS

1. Reflect on the books title for a moment. What are your thoughts

2. After reading the letters submitted to Mary, share your perspective.

3. Now that you have read the book and had time to reflect on all dynamics, how did each interview impact you?

   A. Ethan
   B. Drayke
   C. Zayven
   D. Zack
   E. Brion

4. Identify the wisdom you gained as it pertains to men and how they love?

5. Identify the wisdom you gained pertaining to men and how they cope with loss/pain/betrayal?

6. How has your perception of men and how they love been impacted?

7. What role does societal norms and culture play?

8. In your honest opinion do men love profoundly?

9. Finally, the most provocative question, have you been a benefactor of such profoundness? If yes, how did that level of profoundness nourish your soul?

Be good to yourself,
And love deeply,
Mary E. Gilder

Word of Hello

*R*ecently, I shared conversation with an individual who referred to what we writers do as a hobby. This thinking is very much reflective of how numerous individuals view the ARTS (Actors, Writers, Authors, and Creators of Music, etc.) as indulging in a hobby or not living up to our fullest potential.

My belief is that we are all here on assignment and GOD has blessed each of us with various gifts and talents. There is an assignment you were sent here to share with the world on some level. Being the imperfect humans that we are, we place a value on each assignment.

Some assignments may produce enormous wealth, yet no tangible wealth is attached to the assignment of others. However, they share equal value because the assignment comes from our Creator. I often share how as a 7th grader, I came to understand that regardless of my many life accomplishments, my assignment from GOD was to bring about enlightenment with my written words.

Reflect on this: if writers and authors put down their pens and turned off their lap tops, how would our world be impacted? How would your life be directly impacted? Without doubt you could forget about watching your favorite television shows, going to the movies, reading books, magazines and newspapers. And let's not forget about the purchasing and downloading of music. Also, time spent at the theater and your local art galleries would cease to exist. Yes, so much of what we authors and writers do impact your life in ways you may take for granted.

A word of advice to my readers: make a commitment to invest time in connecting with your own assignment. And when you make that connection, you will come to understand that true power and wealth is measured in something more profound than dollars and cents. I believe it to be housed in every step traveled in your journey.

With that said, I take nothing for granted. Especially the support extended to me from my readers. You have been so good to me and I'm inspired to give to you nothing less than my very best. And I will continue to do just that.

I extend to you my deepest appreciation.

Much Love,

Mary E. Gilder

About the Author

M ary E. Gilder was born and reared in the beautiful city of San Diego, California. A proud graduate of Samuel Morse High School, she went on to earn a Bachelor of Science and a Master's Degree from San Diego State University, as well as recognition from the National Association of Women, for her scholarly achievements. As of recently, Mary was honored by the Northern California African American Museum and Library for her contribution in American history and culture. In addition, she was celebrated by the Association of African American Women for her literary contribution and highlighted in *Redbook* magazine.

Along with being an author, Mary is a Licensed Clinical Therapist, Consultant, Human Rights Activist and a Speaker.

Mary continues to reside in Northern California and is at work on the screen play for, *Even a Man Can Have a Broken Heart.*

Visit her website at www.maryegilder.com.

In memory of my beautiful father
who is deeply missed

Mr. Harvey Wilson jr.
November 9, 1942 - October 6, 2008

CPSIA information can be obtained
at www.ICGtesting.com
Printed in the USA
FSOW01n0308200715
8975FS